Latimer Foundations 10

The Athanasian Creed

Martin Davie

The Latimer Trust

'The Athanasian Creed' © Martin Davie 2019. All rights reserved.

ISBN 978-1-906327-58-3

Cover photo: 'Vector illustration for Christian community: Holy Trinity. Trinity symbol' by tatadonets.

Published by the Latimer Trust August 2019.

The Latimer Trust (formerly Latimer House, Oxford) is a conservative Evangelical research organisation within the Church of England, whose main aim is to promote the history and theology of Anglicanism as understood by those in the Reformed tradition. Interested readers are welcome to consult its website for further details of its many activities.

The Latimer Trust

London N14 4PS UK

Registered Charity: 1084337

Company Number: 4104465

Web: www.latimertrust.org

E-mail: administrator@latimertrust.org

Views expressed in works published by The Latimer Trust are those of the authors and do not necessarily represent the official position of The Latimer Trust.

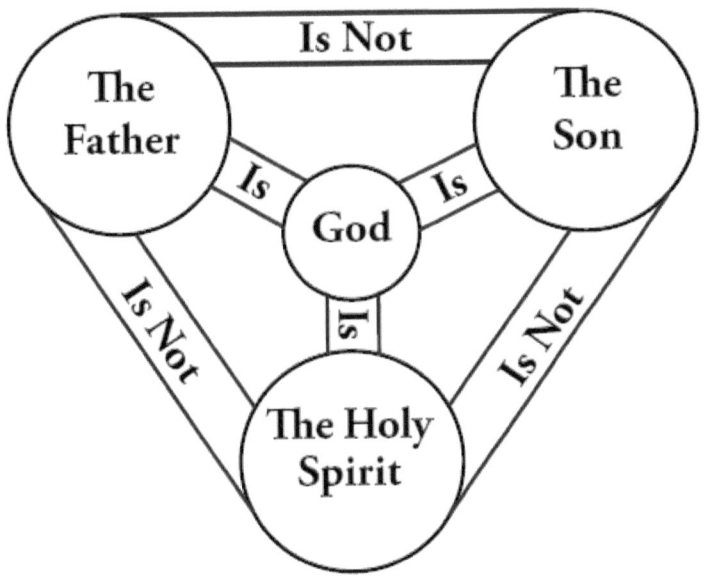

Contents Page

Introduction: The Neglected Creed..4

1. What is the Athanasian Creed?..6

2. The History of the Athanasian Creed...18

3. The Theology of the Athanasian Creed..45

4. Why the Athanasian Creed still matters..84

5. Using the Athanasian Creed today..89

6. Appendix 1: The Athanasian Creed from *English Prayer Book*...........94

7. Appendix 2: A Lutheran Antiphonal version of the Athanasian Creed 97

8. Bibliography..101

Introduction: The Neglected Creed

There have been three creeds which the Western Church has historically regarded as theologically authoritative and which it has used in its worship: the Apostles' Creed, the Nicene Creed and the Athanasian Creed.

The Church of England has traditionally been one with the rest of the Western Church on this matter. Article VIII of the *Thirty-Nine Articles* affirms the authority of all three creeds, declaring that they 'ought thoroughly to be received and believed: for they may be proved by most certain warrants of holy Scripture.' The *Book of Common Prayer* makes provision for all three creeds to be regularly used in Church of England worship, the Apostles' Creed at Morning and Evening Prayer, the Nicene Creed at Holy Communion and the Athanasian Creed in place of the Apostles' Creed at Morning Prayer thirteen times a year.[1]

At first sight the position of the Athanasian Creed in the Church of England appears to remain unchanged. The affirmation of the Athanasian Creed by Article VIII still remains the Church of England's official position with regard to its authority and provision is still made both in the *Book of Common Prayer* and in *Common Worship*[2] for the Athanasian Creed to be used in Church of England services. However, in reality the Athanasian Creed has become the neglected creed.

As we shall see, from the end of the seventeenth century critics of the Creed have objected to its use by the Church of England on various grounds, including that it was not, as traditionally thought, the work of

---

[1] The rubric at the beginning of the Athanasian Creed in the *Book of Common Prayer* declares: Upon these Feasts; Christmas Day, the Epiphany, Saint Matthias, Easter Day, Ascension Day, Whitsunday, Saint John Baptist, Saint James, Saint Bartholomew, Saint Matthew, Saint Simon and Saint Jude, Saint Andrew, and upon Trinity Sunday, shall be sung or said at Morning Prayer, instead of the Apostles' Creed, this Confession of our Christian Faith, commonly called the Creed of Saint Athanasius, by the Minister and people standing.'
[2] *Common Worship* lays down that 'At a celebration of Holy Communion, the Apostles' Creed or the Athanasian Creed in an authorized form may be used in place of the Nicene Creed.'

Introduction: The Neglected Creed

Athanasius of Alexandria, that its theology was excessively severe in that it consigned to eternal damnation everyone who did not subscribe to every detail of its teaching, and that its language was too complex for general congregational use. Such objections were, however, countered by defenders of the Creed who argued that it was a necessary bulwark of Christian orthodoxy, and they did not lead the Church of England to change its official position.

Nevertheless, during the course of the twentieth century the Athanasian Creed gradually dropped out of regular use in the Church of England. As a result, the position in the Church of England today is that the Apostles' and Nicene Creeds are generally very well known, their theology is for the most part relatively well understood and they are regularly used in services. By contrast, the Athanasian Creed is relatively unknown, its theology is not well understood even by the clergy, and it is almost never used in services.

The purpose of this little book is to seek to counter this neglect of the Athanasian Creed. It is in five chapters.

Chapter 1, 'What is the Athanasian Creed?' gives the text of the Creed in English and the original Latin and explains what sort of document it is.

Chapter 2, 'The History of the Athanasian Creed,' explains what we know about where and when the Creed was written, who wrote it, why it was written, and how it came to be used throughout the Western Church.

Chapter 3, 'The Theology of the Athanasian Creed,' goes through the text section by section, explaining what it teaches and why what it teaches is true.

Chapter 4, 'Why the Athanasian Creed Still Matters,' explains why the Creed still matters, not only because of its importance in the history of Christian theology and liturgy, but primarily because of the truthfulness of its teaching.

Chapter 5, 'Using the Athanasian Creed today,' explores how people in the Church of England today can be encouraged to make use of the Creed.

1. What is the Athanasian Creed?

The Text of the Creed

The English version of the Athanasian Creed according to the *Book of Common Prayer*

The Creed in the original Latin[3]

¹Whosoever will be saved: before all things it is necessary that he hold the Catholick Faith. ²Which Faith except every one do keep whole and undefiled: without doubt he shall perish everlastingly.

¹Quicunque vult salvus esse, ante omnia opus est, ut teneat catholicam fidem: ²Quam nisi quis integram inviolatamque servaverit, absque dubio in aeternum peribit.

³And the Catholick Faith is this: That we worship one God in Trinity, and Trinity in Unity; ⁴Neither confounding the Persons: nor dividing the Substance. ⁵For there is one Person of the Father, another of the Son: and another of the Holy Ghost. ⁶But the Godhead of the Father, of the Son, and of the Holy Ghost, is all one: the Glory equal, the Majesty co-eternal.

³Fides autem catholica haec est, ut unum Deum in trinitate, et trinitatem in unitate veneremur, ⁴neque confundentes personas neque substantiam separantes. ⁵Alia est enim persona Patris, alia Filii, alia Spiritus sancti; ⁶sed Patris et Filii et Spiritus sancti una est divinitas, aequalis gloria, coaeterna maiestas.

---

[3] The Latin text is the critical edition contained in J. N. D. Kelly, *The Athanasian Creed* (London: A&C Black, 1964), 17-20.

⁷Such as the Father is, such is the Son: and such is the Holy Ghost. ⁸The Father uncreate, the Son uncreate: and the Holy Ghost uncreate. ⁹The Father incomprehensible, the Son incomprehensible: and the Holy Ghost incomprehensible. ¹⁰The Father eternal, the Son eternal: and the Holy Ghost eternal. ¹¹And yet they are not three eternals: but one eternal. ¹²As also there are not three incomprehensibles, nor three uncreated: but one uncreated, and one incomprehensible. ¹³So likewise the Father is Almighty, the Son Almighty: and the Holy Ghost Almighty. ¹⁴And yet they are not three Almighties: but one Almighty.

¹⁵So the Father is God, the Son is God: and the Holy Ghost is God. ¹⁶And yet they are not three Gods: but one God. ¹⁷So likewise the Father is Lord, the Son Lord: and the Holy Ghost Lord. ¹⁸And yet not three Lords: but one Lord. ¹⁹For like as we are compelled by the Christian verity: to acknowledge every Person by himself to be God and Lord; ²⁰So are we forbidden by the Catholick Religion: to say there be three Gods, or three Lords.

²¹The Father is made of none: neither created, nor begotten. ²²The Son is of the Father alone: not made, nor created, but begotten. ²³The Holy Ghost is of

⁷Qualis Pater, talis Filius, talis et Spiritus sanctus. ⁸Increatus Pater, increatus Filius, increatus Spiritus sanctus. ⁹Immensus Pater, immensus Filius, immensus Spiritus sanctus; ¹⁰aeternus Pater, aeternus Filius, aeternus Spiritus sanctus: ¹¹et tamen non tres aeterni, sed unus aeternus; ¹²sicut non tres increati nec tres immensi, sed unus increatus, et unus immensus. ¹³Similiter omnipotens Pater, omnipotens Filius, omnipotens Spiritus sanctus; ¹⁴et tamen non tres omnipotentes, sed unus omnipotens.

¹⁵Ita deus Pater, deus Filius, deus Spiritus sanctus; ¹⁶et tamen non tres dii, sed unus est deus. ¹⁷Ita dominus Pater, dominus Filius, dominus Spiritus sanctus; ¹⁸et tamen non tres domini, sed unus est dominus. ¹⁹Quia, sicut singillatim unamquamque personam et deum et dominum confiteri christiana veritate compellimur, ²⁰ita tres deos aut dominos dicere catholica religione prohibemur.

²¹Pater a nullo est factus nec creatus nec genitus. ²²Filius a Patre solo est, non factus nec creatus sed genitus. ²³Spiritus sanctus a Patre et Filio, non

the Father and of the Son: neither made, nor created, nor begotten, but proceeding. [24]So there is one Father, not three Fathers; one Son, not three Sons: one Holy Ghost, not three Holy Ghosts. [25]And in this Trinity none is afore, or after other: none is greater, or less than another; [26]But the whole three Persons are co-eternal together: and co-equal. [27]So that in all things, as is aforesaid: the Unity in Trinity, and the Trinity in Unity is to be worshipped. [28]He therefore that will be saved: must thus think of the Trinity.

[29]Furthermore it is necessary to everlasting salvation: that he also believe rightly the Incarnation of our Lord Jesus Christ. [30]For the right Faith is that we believe and confess: that our Lord Jesus Christ, the Son of God, is God and Man.

[31]God, of the Substance of the Father, begotten before the worlds: and Man, of the Substance of his Mother, born in the world; [32]Perfect God, and Perfect Man: of a reasonable soul and human flesh subsisting; [33]Equal to the Father, as touching his Godhead: and inferior to the Father, as touching his Manhood.

[34]Who although he be God and Man: yet he is not two, but one

factus nec creatus nec genitus sed procedens. [24]Unus ergo Pater, non tres Patres; unus Filius, non tres Filii; unus Spiritus sanctus, non tres Spiritus sancti. [25]Et in hac trinitate nihil prius aut posterius, nihil maius aut minus, [26]sed totae tres personae coaeternae sibi sunt et coaequales. [27]Ita ut per omnia, sicut iam supra dictum est, et trinitas in unitate et unitas in trinitate veneranda sit. [28]Qui vult ergo salvus esse, ita de trinitate sentiat.

[29]Sed necessarium est ad aeternam salutem ut incarnationem quoque domini nostri Iesu Christi fideliter credat. [30]Est ergo fides recta ut credamus et confiteamur, quia dominus noster Iesus Christus Dei Filius et deus pariter et homo est.

[31]Deus est ex substantia Patris ante saecula genitus, et homo est ex substantia matris in saeculo natus; [32]perfectus deus, perfectus homo, ex anima rationabili et humana carne subsistens; [33]aequalis Patri secundum divinitatem, minor Patri secundum humanitatem.

[34]Qui licet Deus sit et homo, non duo tamen sed unus est Christus.

Christ; ³⁵One, not by conversion of the Godhead into flesh: but by taking of the Manhood into God; ³⁶One altogether, not by confusion of Substance: but by unity of Person. ³⁷For as the reasonable soul and flesh is one man: so God and Man is one Christ.

³⁸Who suffered for our salvation: descended into hell, rose again the third day from the dead. ³⁹He ascended into heaven, he sitteth on the right hand of the Father, God Almighty: from whence he shall come to judge the quick and the dead. ⁴⁰At whose coming all men shall rise again with their bodies: and shall give account for their own works. ⁴¹And they that have done good shall go into life everlasting: and they that have done evil into everlasting fire.

⁴²This is the Catholick Faith: which except a man believe faithfully, he cannot be saved.

³⁵Unus autem non conversione divinitatis in carne, sed adsumptione humanitatis in deo; ³⁶Unus omnino non confusione substantiae, sed unitate personae. ³⁷Nam sicut anima rationabilis et caro unus est homo, ita deus et homo unus est Christus.

³⁸Qui passus est pro salute nostra, descendit ad infera, surrexit a mortuis, ³⁹ascendit ad caelos, sedit ad dexteram Patris, inde venturus judicare vivos et mortuos: ⁴⁰ad cuius adventum omnes homines resurgere habent cum corporibus suis et reddituri sunt de factis propriis rationem; ⁴¹et qui bona egerunt ibunt in vitam aeternam, qui mala in ignem aeternum.

⁴²Haec est fides catholica: quam nisi quis fideliter firmiterque crediderit, salvus esse non poterit.

The Language of the Creed

As indicated in the headings to the text of the Creed given above, the Athanasian Creed is a document that was originally written in Latin. In the words of the eighteenth-century scholar Daniel Waterland:

> The style and phraseology of the Creed, its early reception among the Latins, while unknown to the Greeks; the antiquity and number of the Latin manuscripts, and their

agreement (for the most part) with each other, compared with the lateness, the scarceness, and the disagreement of the Greek copies, all concur to demonstrate that this Creed is originally a Latin composure, rather than a Greek one: and as to any other language besides these two, none is pretended.[4]

Not only is the Athanasian Creed a Latin text, but it is also a particular kind of Latin text.

First, it is a text that is carefully written in a consistent form of rhythmic Latin prose in which the rhythm is based both on the use of long and short syllables (quantitative or metrical rhythm) and on where the emphasis falls when the text is read aloud (accentual rhythm). The fact that the rhythmic scheme is a consistent throughout suggests that it has always been a unified text and that it was written (or at least edited) by a single hand. The combination of a metrical and accentual rhyme scheme with an emphasis on the accentual suggests that the text was composed in the period from the middle of the fourth to the middle of the sixth centuries when these two rhyme schemes tended to overlap and the fact that the accentual scheme predominates suggests it was composed in the second half of this period.[5]

It has sometimes been suggested that the rhythmic structure of the Athanasian Creed means that it was composed for use as a canticle or hymn. As we shall see, it came to be used in this way from the early Middle Ages onwards, however the rhythmic structure present in the Creed does not in itself show that it was composed for this purpose. As John Kelly notes, the rhythmic forms present in it were those 'considered appropriate by careful writers for sermons, letters, formal treatises etc., where no question of singing arose.'[6]

Secondly, it is a text whose vocabulary and grammar are those of later rather than classical Latin, which fits in with the dating suggested by its

---

[4] Daniel Waterland, *A Critical History of the Athanasian Creed*, (London: Forgotten Books, 2015), 46.
[5] For studies of the rhyme scheme in the Athanasian Creed see A. E. Burn, *An Introduction to the Creeds and to the Te Deum* (London: Methuen, 1899), 248–257, and Kelly, *The Athanasian Creed*, 60–65.
[6] Kelly, *The Athanasian Creed*, 65.

rhythmic structure. Examples include the use of *totae* with the sense of *omnes* 'all' in verse 26, the use of word *rationabilis* ('reasonable') instead of the more correct *rationalis* in verses 32 and 37 and the use of the verb *habere* ('to have') with the present infinitive to express the future in verse 40.[7]

Thirdly, it is a text that has parallels in both thought and language with the works of a number of Christian writers from the fourth to the sixth centuries. Three examples will serve to illustrate this.[8]

- The words of verses 17 and 18 of the Athanasian Creed, 'So likewise the Father is Lord, the Son Lord: and the Holy Ghost Lord. And yet not three Lords: but one Lord' (*Ita dominus Pater, dominus Filius, dominus Spiritus sanctus; et tamen non tres domini, sed unus est dominus*), parallel the statement by Ambrose of Milan (339–397) 'Both the Father is Lord and the Son is Lord ... yet not two lords but one Lord' (*Et pater dominus, et filius dominus ... et non duo domini, sed unus dominus*).[9]
- The words of verses 13 and 14, 'So likewise the Father is Almighty, the Son Almighty: and the Holy Ghost Almighty. And yet they are not three Almighties: but one Almighty' (*Similiter omnipotens Pater, omnipotens Filius, omnipotens Spiritus sanctus; et tamen non tres omnipotentes, sed unus omnipotens*, parallel the statement by Augustine of Hippo (354–430) 'So the Father is omnipotent, the Son is omnipotent and the Holy Spirit is omnipotent; yet not three omnipotents, but one omnipotent' (*Itaque omnipotens pater, omnipotens filius, omnipotens spiritus sanctus; nec tamen tres omnipotentes, sed unus omnipotens*).[10]
- The words of verse 15 and 16, 'So the Father is God, the Son is God: and the Holy Ghost is God. And yet they are not three Gods: but one God ' (*Ita deus Pater, deus Filius, deus Spiritus sanctus; et tamen non tres dii, sed unus est deus*), parallel the statement by Caesarius of Arles (c. 468–542) 'The Father is God, the Son is God, and the Holy Spirit is God, yet there are not three gods but

---

[7] For details see Kelly, *The Athanasian Creed*, 67–69.
[8] For further parallels see Kelly, *The Athanasian Creed*, 24–33.
[9] Ambrose of Milan, *Commentary on Luke*, 10:4,
[10] Augustine of Hippo, *On the Trinity*, 5:9.

one God' (*Deus pater, deus filius, deus et spiritus sanctus; sed tamen non tres dii, sed unus deus*).'[11]

These kinds of parallels locate the text in the late Patristic period, in the same way that parallels with the language and thought of Luther and Calvin would suggest a date for a text in the Reformation or immediate post-Reformation period. They also raise the question of the authorship of the text (do any of the parallels suggest joint authorship?) to which we will return in the next chapter. Finally, they indicate that the theology put forward in the text is not idiosyncratic, but is instead representative of the wider development of orthodox Christian theology at the time when it was written.

The Structure of the Creed

The Athanasian Creed is a text with a very clear structure. It is made up of forty-two verses, each of which focuses on a particular idea. Thus verse 5 states 'there is one Person of the Father, another of the Son: and another of the Holy Ghost,' verse 21 states 'The Father is made of none: neither created, nor begotten,' and verse 37 states 'as the reasonable soul and flesh is one man: so God and Man is one Christ.'

These forty-two verses begin in verses 1 and 2 with the declaration that adherence to the Catholic faith is necessary for salvation:

> Whosoever will be saved: before all things it is necessary that he hold the Catholick Faith. Which Faith except every one do keep whole and undefiled: without doubt he shall perish everlastingly.

Verses 3–41 then describe what the Catholic faith is and finally verse 42 acts as a bookend to the opening two verses by warning the reader that no one can hope for salvation unless they hold to the faith which has just been described: 'This is the Catholick Faith: which except a man believe faithfully, he cannot be saved.'

Verses 3–41 are divided into three sections, verses 3–27 describe right belief concerning the Trinity, verses 30–37 describe right belief concerning the person of Christ and verses 38–41 describe right belief concerning Christ's death, resurrection and ascension and his coming in

---

[11] Caesarius of Arles, *Sermon* 10:1.

judgement. Verses 28 and 29 serve as a hinge holding together the two main sections on the Trinity and the person of Christ and further emphasising the importance of right belief for salvation.

The bipartite structure of the Athanasian Creed, focusing first on the Trinity, and then on the person and work of Christ, differs from the more familiar tripartite creedal structure found in the Apostles and Nicene Creeds which focuses in turn on the Father, Son and Holy Spirit. The unfamiliarity of the Athanasian Creed's structure led scholars in the nineteenth century to argue that it was not originally a single whole, but that it was constructed by the bringing together of two originally separate documents on Trinitarian theology and Christology in the eighth or ninth centuries.[12]

This argument has now been rejected by students of the Creed. This is because:

a. The Creed is a stylistic unity;
b. The earliest evidence we have for the Creed, going back to the sixth century, is evidence for one document;
c. We know of a family of bipartite creeds, mainly from Spain, and inspired by Gregory of Elivira's *Libellus fidei* from the closing decades of the fourth century, into which the Athanasian Creed fits comfortably.

The structure of the Athanasian Creed only seems odd to us because the existence of this family of creeds has been largely forgotten.[13]

The Title of the Creed

There are two titles which are used for the Athanasian Creed in the Church of England. One is the Athanasian Creed and the other is the *Quiqunque vult*. The first title reflects the traditional association of the Creed with Athanasius, the great fourth-century champion of Trinitarian orthodoxy. The second identifies the Creed by its opening words in Latin, *Quicunque vult salvus esse* ('Whosoever wishes to be saved').

---

[12] See J. R. Lumby, *The History of the Creeds* (Cambridge: Deighton Bell, 1873) and C. A. Swainson, *The Nicene and Apostles' Creeds* (London: John Murray, 1875).
[13] For detail on this point see Kelly, *The Athanasian Creed*, 55-59.

Neither of these appears to be the original title of the Creed. The earliest titles we have for the Creed date from a collection of homilies produced on the instruction of Caesarius, Bishop of Arles in what is now southern France, but was then Gaul, at some point in the first half of the sixth century. In this text, which is contained in a Latin manuscript called the *Zwiefalten Codex* dating from about 1100,[14] a version of the Creed is included as one of the homilies. In the list of contents this homily is listed as 'The faith of Saint Athanasius' (*Fides Sancti Athanasii*) and in the text it is given the title 'The Catholic faith of Saint Athanasius, Bishop' (*Fides Catholica Sancti Athanasii Episcopii*).

The second title is an expansion of the first and the point that they are both making is that the contents of the homily express the orthodox ('Catholic') faith as taught by Athanasius. The central tenet of Athanasius' teaching was that our salvation was made possible because God himself became incarnate in Jesus Christ[15] and it is the two fundamental truths underlying this teaching, that God is Triune and that Jesus Christ is both divine and human, that are taught by the Athanasian Creed.

What these titles are probably not saying is that the Creed was written by Athanasius himself. As we shall see in the next chapter, if Caesarius did not write the Creed it was produced by someone in his circle, and he would have been responsible for the titles given to it in the collection of homilies. We know that Caesarius was in the habit of attributing to Fathers from the past homilies which he had written on the grounds that they expressed the theology of the Father concerned. This would make it likely that, in a similar way, the titles in the collection of homilies are not an attempt to identify the author of the Creed, but rather (as indicated in the previous paragraph) an attempt to say something about its contents. A good modern analogy would be the practice of calling pieces of theology 'Lutheran' or 'Barthian' meaning not that they were written by Martin Luther or Karl Barth, but that they reflect their key theological emphases.

---

[14] See G. Morin, 'L'Origine du symbole d'Athanase: temoignage inedit de s. Cesaire d'Arles,' *Revue Benedictine*, XLIV (1932); 207-219.
[15] See Athanasius, *On the Incarnation of the Word*, In the *Nicene and Post-Nicene Fathers* (Edinburgh and Grand Rapids: T&T Clark/Eerdmans, 1998), 31-67.

The Purpose of the Creed

We do not have an explanation from the author of the Creed concerning its purpose. In the absence of such an explanation we have to work out the purpose of the Creed from the Creed itself.

We can do this in two stages. We can start by saying what the purpose of the Creed is not and having done this we can then say what the purpose of the Creed is.

Starting with what the purpose of the Creed is not, we can say first of all that it is not intended as a confession of faith (even though this is how it has subsequently come to be used). The Apostles' and Nicene Creeds are intended to be individual and communal confessions of faith. That is why they say 'I believe' and 'we believe.' This confessional element is absent from the Athanasian Creed.

Secondly, it is not a polemical piece of writing intended to give a detailed criticism and rebuttal of theological error. It makes clear that there are certain things that we should not say. Thus verse 24 declares 'So there is one Father, not three Fathers; one Son, not three Sons: one Holy Ghost, not three Holy Ghosts' and verse 35 states that Jesus Christ is one person 'not by conversion of the Godhead into flesh: but by taking of the Manhood into God.' However, unlike polemical works such as Athanasius' *Orations against the Arians*,[16] or Augustine's *Anti-Pelagian Treatises*,[17] the Athanasian Creed does not go into any details about the reasons why saying these things is wrong and why the arguments put forward in their favour do not hold water.

Thirdly, just as it is not a polemical piece of writing, so also it is not an apologetic piece of writing. It states what it thinks the Catholic faith is and why it is important to hold to it, but it never seeks to persuade people that

---

[16] See Athanasius, *The Orations of St Athanasius against the Arians*, (London: Macmillan, 1873).
[17] See Augustine, *Anti-Pelagian Writings*, in the *Nicene and Post-Nicene Fathers* (Edinburgh and Grand Rapids: T&T Clark/Eerdmans, 1997).

its view of the Catholic faith and its importance is correct. It never says 'This is why you should believe these things.'[18]

Fourthly, the Athanasian Creed is not intended to be a sermon. It is not written to address the hearts and minds of a congregation so that they come to believe and do certain things. Sermons are written to address a particular group of people, but the Athanasian Creed is not addressed to anyone in particular. It does not say '*you* should do this if you want to be saved,' but rather '*whoever* wants to be saved should do this.'

In the *Zwiefalten Codex* an attempt is made to make the text more like a sermon by adding the word *fratres*, 'brothers,' at the end of the first clause so that it reads 'whoever wants to be saved, brothers.'[19] However, this addition is not part of the original text and it leaves the rest of the text still resolutely un-sermon like.

So, if the Athanasian Creed was not written to be a confession of faith, a piece of polemic, a work of apologetics, or a sermon, then what was its purpose? A clue is provided in the Preface in the *Zwiefalten Codex* which declares:

> And because it is necessary that all clergymen, and laymen too, should be familiar with the Catholic faith, we have first of all written out in this collection the Catholic faith itself as the holy fathers defined it, for we ought both ourselves frequently to read it and to instruct others in it.[20]

As what we call the Athanasian Creed immediately follows this Preface, it is clear that 'the Catholic faith itself as the holy fathers defined it' is the Creed and, as Kelly observes, this tells us that:

> ... in the eyes of Caesarius and his contemporaries, the creed was not, apparently, a liturgical piece, but a concise

---

[18] See by way of comparison an apologetic work such as Athenagoras, *A Plea for the Christians* in *The Ante-Nicene Fathers* (Edinburgh and Grand Rapids: T&T Clark/Eerdmans, 2001), 123–148.
[19] For this addition see Kelly, *The Athanasian Creed*, 129.
[20] Kelly, *The Athanasian Creed*, 36.

summary of orthodox teaching to be studied and mastered by the faithful.[21]

In the absence of direct testimony by its author we cannot be absolutely sure that the Creed was written to provide such a summary, but this seems extremely likely as it corresponds to what we find in the text of the Creed itself. The text is a short piece of Christian instruction, addressed to all Christians, that takes its readers one step at a time through why right ('Catholic') faith matters and what right faith involves in relation to the Trinity and the person and work of Christ. As the Preface says, it explains the faith as defined by the 'holy fathers' (that is, the orthodox Fathers of the fourth and fifth centuries) and it explains it in a way that is clear, concise, and easy to teach and memorise, since each verse makes a specific point.

Although it is different in form, the Athanasian Creed thus appears to have had a similar purpose to the catechisms of the Reformation period, such as Luther's *Shorter Catechism* or the Catechism in the *Book of Common Prayer,* in that it was written to provide an instructional tool to help clergy and laity learn and teach the basics of the Christian faith.

---

[21] Kelly, *The Athanasian Creed*, 37.

2. The History of the Athanasian Creed

Where was the Creed written?

Since the rise of critical study of the origins of the Creed in the sixteenth century a general consensus has emerged that the Creed was composed in what is now southern France, but was then Gaul. Thus Waterland states 'There is great reason to believe that this Creed was made in Gaul.'[22] Thus also Harold Browne writes 'As to the place where it was made, evidence tends to show that it was Gaul'[23] and more recently Gerald Bray declares that it 'was probably produced in Southern Gaul.'[24]

There are a number of pieces of evidence which point to Gaul as the Creed's point of origin.

- First, the fact that the Creed was written in Latin rather than in Greek or Syriac indicates that it was written in what had been the Western half of the Roman Empire, that is to say in Western Europe or North Africa. In addition, there are numerous parallels between the kind of Latin used in the Creed and that found in writers from Gaul.
- Secondly, as we have noted, the bipartite structure of the Creed belongs to a family of creeds originating in Spain and there were very close links between the churches in Spain and Gaul.
- Thirdly, as we have also noted, the earliest evidence for the Creed comes from a collection of homilies produced at the behest of St. Caeasarius, who was Bishop of Arles in Southern Gaul.
- Fourthly, there are strong parallels in thought and language between the contents of the Creed and the language and theology of three writers associated with the great monastery at Lerins off the coast of Southern Gaul, Caesarius, Faustus of Riez (c 405–495) and Vincent of Lerins (d 445). Theologians associated with this monastery combined support for the Trinitarian theology of Augustine with an emphasis on the importance of human volition and responsibility, and it is this combination that we also find in the Athanasian Creed.

---

[22] Waterland, *A Critical History*, 114.
[23] Harold Browne, *An Exposition of the Thirty Nine Articles* (London: John Parker, 1860), 223.
[24] Gerald Bray, *The Faith We Confess* (London: Latimer Trust, 2009), 57.

- Fifthly, as we shall see in more detail below, the earliest evidence for the Creed after the homily book of Caesarius comes from Gaul and Spain, and the Creed first came into widespread use in Gaul in the eighth and ninth centuries both as a tool for educating the clergy and as part of the liturgy. In addition the Creed makes an early appearance in commentaries and Psalters stemming from Gaul.

When was the Creed written?

In the previous chapter we noted a series of indications about when the Athanasian Creed was written.

We noted that the vocabulary and grammar of the text and the rhyme scheme that it employs all suggest that it was written at some point in the fourth to sixth centuries, and probably in the second half of that period. We further noted that this date for the Creed's composition is also suggested by the parallels in thought and language between the Creed and the writings of theologians from this period and by the fact that the bipartite structure of the Creed places it within a family of creeds that developed from the late fourth century onwards.

The fact that there is a version of the Creed in the collection of sermons contained in the *Zwiefalten Codex* provides another, more precise, indication of its date. Because this collection was put together at the instruction of St. Caesarius it follows that the Creed was written before his death in 542.

542 is thus the very latest that the Creed could have been written. This leaves the question of when was the earliest it could have been written.

The first point to note in this regard is that the Creed's teaching about the Trinity in verses 3–27 reflects the Trinitarian theology expounded by Augustine in his work *On the Trinity*. This work was published in about 417 and this suggests a date for the Athanasian Creed later than 420 in order to allow time for Augustine's work to be 'read, considered, approved, and to gain a general esteem.'[25]

It could, of course, be argued that the relationship between the Creed and the work of St. Augustine was the other way around, with Augustine

---

[25] Waterland, *A Critical History*, 102.

making use of the Creed. However, as Waterland explains, it is much more likely that the work of Augustine came first:

> Creeds and other the like formularies which are to be put into every one's hands, and spread round about, ought not to contain any thing till it has been maturely weighed, long considered, and fully explained, as well as proved, and generally acknowledged by the Churches of Christ. It is therefore much more reasonable to assume that St. Austin's writings should go first, and a general approbation of them in that particular; and then the Creed might conveniently follow, the way being now opened for it.[26]

Secondly, the fact that the teaching of the Creed about the person of Christ in verses 31–37 includes a rejection of the Nestorian heresy, which was condemned at the Council of Ephesus in 431, and that there is a very clear overlap in thought and language between the teaching of the Creed and two writings by Vincent of Lerins, the *Commonitorium* and the *Excerpta,* which are dated c 434–440, both suggest that the Creed was written sometime after the mid-430s.[27]

Once again, the suggestion could be made that Vincent made use of the Creed, but the point made by Waterland about the relationship between Augustine and the Creed would also apply in the case of Vincent. In this case as well it is much more reasonable to suppose that Vincent's work came first and was subsequently made use of by the writer of the Creed as a generally accepted piece of orthodox theology.

Thirdly, as Kelly argues, the language of the Christological section of the Creed is best explained if the Creed was written not only after the mid-430s, but towards the end of the fifth century or at the beginning of the sixth. This is because the tone of this section suggests that it was written sometime after the fierce controversies about Christology in the middle years of the fifth century had had time to die down:

> As a summary of Catholic belief it naturally defends the orthodox line with meticulous care and sets its face firmly

---

[26] Waterland, *A Critical History*, 102–103. Waterland shortens Augustine to 'Austin' in accordance with eighteenth-century practice.
[27] Kelly, *The Athanasian Creed*, 116–117.

against deviations. But the avoidance of the technical jargon of controversy and the absence of anathemas are noticeable. There is nothing decisive, of course, in this feature, but on the whole it seems more consistent with a period when the fires of Christological debate had died down than when they were burning fiercely. A date in the latter part of the 5th century, or round about 500, would seem indicated; and this would agree well with (i) the evidence of the rhythms employed by the creed, and (ii) the degree to which its language has been affected by the growth of vulgar Latin.[28]

Fourthly, the fact that the Creed was included in Caesarius' homily collection as an authorised exposition of the Catholic faith to be used for the instruction of both clergy and laity suggests that by the time of its inclusion the Creed had had been in existence for a sufficient length of time to allow it to gain authority and acceptance as a helpful statement of Christian orthodoxy. On the other hand, the fact that the version included in the text is an edited version suggests that it was not a document that was so old that its wording had become sacrosanct.

Caesarius was Bishop of Arles from 502–42. If the Creed was written at the end of the fifth or the beginning of the sixth century and then included by him in his homily collection in the middle years of his episcopate this would explain why the Creed was sufficiently old to have become accepted as authoritative, but not so old that its wording was sacrosanct.

Taken together, the evidence we possess thus points to a date for the composition of the Athanasian Creed at the end of the fifth or the beginning of the sixth century.

Who Wrote the Creed?

The view universally held in the Middle Ages was that the Creed was written by Athanasius himself. This view of its authorship continued to be defended in the sixteenth century. Richard Hooker declares, for instance, in *The Laws of Ecclesiastical Polity* that the Creed was written by Athanasius in about 340 as part of his struggle against the Arian heresy

---

[28] Kelly, *The Athanasian Creed*, 112–113.

and having been presented to Pope Julius I and the Emperor Jovian 'was both in the East and West accepted as a treasure of inestimable price.'[29]

Even at the time Hooker was writing, however, the Athanasian authorship of the Creed had begun to be questioned, and during the seventeenth century it came to be generally abandoned. Thus in his lectures on the Apostles' Creed published in 1659 John Pearson refers to the Creed 'commonly attributed to Athanasius' and then goes on to write 'as it was confessed to be first written in Latin, so it is most probable that it was composed by some member of the Latin church.'[30]

In this quotation Pearson puts his finger on the key issue that led people to reject Athanasian authorship, namely that it was a Latin text and therefore most likely composed by a Latin speaking author, whereas Athanasius was Greek speaking and wrote his works in Greek. If we add to this consideration what else we know about the provenance and likely date of the Creed then Athanasian authorship can be completely ruled out. Athanasius was a fourth century bishop and theologian (his dates are c 296–373) who came from Egypt. By contrast, as we have seen, the author of the Athanasian Creed seems to have been someone from southern Gaul writing at the turn of the fifth and sixth centuries.[31]

If the Creed was not written by Athanasius, then who did write it? Since the seventeenth century numerous answers have been given to this question.[32] Suggestions have included Ambrose, Hilary of Arles (403–449) and Fulgentius of Ruspe in North Africa (c 462–c 533), but all three of these are unlikely either for reasons of dating, or geography, or both. If the evidence we have considered above is to be believed, what we are looking for is someone who wrote in Latin, in Gaul, at the end of the fifth

---

[29] Richard Hooker, *The Laws of Ecclesiastical Polity*, Book V, XLIII:6,
[30] John Pearson, *An Exposition of the Creed*, Art XVIII (London: George Bell, 1902), 492.
[31] It is worth noting that the reformed Church of England did not commit itself to Athanasian authorship of the Creed. In the rubric to the Creed in the Book of Common Prayer it is referred to as 'this Confession of our Christian Faith, commonly called the Creed of St Athanasius, 'a description which leaves the question of authorship open.
[32] See Waterland, *A Critical History*, 4–23 and Kelly, *The Athanasian Creed*, 3–14.

or the beginning of the sixth century, and who was in the orbit of the monastery of Lerins.

Someone who would fit all these criteria is Caesarius himself and he has been suggested as the author of the Creed.[33] However, as Kelly notes, there are three important arguments against this suggestion.

First, he says the formula *fides catholica* (the Catholic faith) which is used to describe the Creed in the Zwiefalten collection militates against Caesarian authorship:

> One's first impulse is to interpret it as denoting a statement of belief which Caesarius assumes to be familiar to his reader, and which both he and they regard with respect. This does not absolutely preclude him from being its author, but renders the supposition somewhat unlikely.[34]

Secondly, there are 'small but significant discrepancies' between the Creed and what we know of the theology of Caesarius from other sources:

> For example, while it explicitly denies (v.23) that the Sprit is 'begotten,' Caesarius seems to have been unsure, in view of the silence of Scripture, whether his procession is a generation or not. Again, where the creed speaks of the Father, Son and Holy Spirit as being each *immensus* ['incomprehensible'] (v.9) it would have been more in accordance with Caesarius's idiom to characterize them as being *ubique* ('everywhere'), since this adverb fitted better with his theory that, being omnipresent, the divine persons could not be 'sent.' Further, the comparison of the hypostatic union to the union of soul and body in man is never used by Caesarius, although he had ample occasion for using it had he wanted to. Finally, it may be questioned whether Caesarius, who abhorred Semi-

---

[33] C. H. Turner, *The History of Creeds and Anathemas in the Early Church* (London: SPCK, 1906), 75–78.
[34] Kelly, *The Athanasian Creed*, 121–122.

Pelagianism, would have stressed the importance of personal decision as the creed does.³⁵

Thirdly, the Zwiefalten version of the text has a number of variations from what text criticism shows to be the original text of the Creed and these are all changes:

> ... from the point of view of elegance of diction, for the worse, betraying what Morin called 'une maladresse de style, une sorte de mefait litterarire.'³⁶ Is it conceivable, he felt reluctantly obliged to ask, that if Caesarius had possessed the stylistic sensitivity and skill to compose this splendid text in the first place, he would then have set about systematically botching it in this unfeeling manner?³⁷

What all this means is that the answer to the question 'Who wrote the creed?' is 'We don't know.' At the moment, barring the discovery of more information, the identity of the individual who originally wrote the Athanasian Creed remains a mystery.

Why Was the Athanasian Creed Written?

If we do not know exactly who wrote the Creed, can we work out why they wrote it? The answer is that we have no direct testimony about the matter. However, the pieces of evidence we do have enable us to piece together a plausible account of why the Creed was written.

As we saw at the end of the previous chapter, the contents of the Creed, and what is said about it in the Preface to the *Zwiefalten Codex* both point to the Creed's having been written as an instructional tool to help clergy and laity teach and learn the basics of the Christian faith.

This raises the further question as to why someone writing in southern Gaul at the end of the fifth or the beginning of the sixth century thought that such an instructional tool was needed. Here we do not have to guess because the Creed itself tells us.

---

³⁵ Kelly, *The Athanasian Creed*, 122.
³⁶ 'A clumsiness of style, a sort of literary misdemeanour.'
³⁷ Kelly, *The Athanasian Creed*, 122–123, quoting Morin, 'L'Origine du symbole d'Athanase,' 217.

As we noted when we looked at the structure of the Creed, in three places in the Creed its author insists on the link between adhering to the Catholic faith and being in a state of salvation. These three places, which have come to be known as the 'damnatory clauses' because they warn about the danger of eternal damnation, are:

- Verses 1 and 2:

'Whosoever will be saved: before all things it is necessary that he hold the Catholick Faith. Which Faith except every one do keep whole and undefiled: without doubt he shall perish everlastingly.'

- Verse 29:

'Furthermore it is necessary to everlasting salvation: that he also believe rightly the Incarnation of our Lord Jesus Christ.'

- Verse 42:

'This is the Catholick Faith: which except a man believe faithfully, he cannot be saved.'

What these verses tell us is that the Creed's author believed that its readers not only needed instruction about the teaching of the Catholic faith concerning the Trinity and the person of Christ, but also about the vital importance for their salvation of adhering to such teaching.

As numerous commentators on the Creed have pointed out, the subject of verses 1 and 2 is not humanity in general, but someone who already holds the Catholic faith. 'That he hold' (*ut teneat*) in verse 1 is equivalent to 'keep' (*servaverit*) in verse 2 and both imply existing possession of the faith in question. As Edgar Gibson explains:

> 'Hold' and 'keep' are not inadequate renderings; but if 'keep' and 'preserve' were substituted for them the drift of the clause would be more sharply brought out; and the English reader would feel at once that the warning is against apostasy, i.e., against letting go that which has been received. It is impossible for a man to 'keep' or 'preserve' that which is nor previously in his possession. It would be an abuse of terms to tell an impure person to 'preserve his chastity.' He cannot do it, for such a phrase

necessarily implies previously innocence and purity. So also when it is said of the Catholic faith that 'except every one do keep [it] whole and undefiled, without doubt he shall perish everlastingly,' it is obvious that the only case contemplated is that of men who have already received it and are in possession of it.'[38]

'Believe rightly' and 'believe faithfully' in verse 29 and 42 need to be understood in the light of verses 1 and 2. What they are talking about is someone who knows the Catholic faith continuing to believe it 'rightly' (i.e. correctly) and 'faithfully' (i.e. loyally).

The historical issue is why the author of the Creed felt it necessary to repeatedly make this point. Why was it so urgent for them that their readers knew the importance of tenaciously holding on to the Catholic faith?

A likely explanation is provided by the fact that at the time the Creed was written southern Gaul was ruled over by the Visigoths, a Germanic people who had crossed the frozen Rhine into the Roman Empire at the start of the fifth century. By the end of the century the Visigoth Kingdom of Toulouse ruled over Gaul south of the Loire and most of what is now Spain and Portugal.[39]

The Goths, having been evangelised in the mid-fourth century by an Arian missionary called Ulfilas, were Arian Christians who held, in the words of Kelly:

> ... that the Son is inferior to the Father and the Spirit in His turn is inferior to the Son. Thus, according to them, there were not only three divine persons (the term 'divine' having a diminished force as applied to the second or the third), but three divine realities too, since all three were in effect different beings.[40]

---

[38] E. C. S. Gibson, *The Thirty Nine Articles of the Church of England* (London: Methuen, 3ed, 1902), 348.
[39] For the Visigoths and the Kingdom of Toulouse see Norman Davies, *Forgotten Kingdoms* (London: Penguin, 2012), Ch. 1.
[40] Kelly, *The Athanasian Creed*, 78.

As Kelly goes on to say:

> Their teaching thus amounted in practice to tritheism, and their Catholic opponents never wearied of upbraiding them with returning to the polytheism of their barbarian background.[41]

For Catholics in southern Gaul there must have been a perennial concern that people would accept the Arian polytheism of the ruling Visigoths, either in the face of persecution, or for reasons of personal advancement, or simply because the concept of three different divine beings seemed easier to understand than Catholic Trinitarianism.

Such a concern would explain why the Creed emphasises the need to remain loyal to Catholic orthodoxy and why the first half of the Creed is concerned with explaining that although there are three different persons in the Godhead there is only one divine reality which all three persons equally possess.

It would also explain why the name of Athanasius was attached to the Creed. Athanasius was revered as somebody who remained loyal to Catholic orthodoxy against Arianism even though this meant clashing with the imperial authorities' support for Arianism and suffering five periods of deposition and exile as a result. Calling the Creed 'The Catholic faith of St. Athanasius' would be a way of saying to its readers: 'This is the faith to which Athanasius of blessed memory remained loyal and for which he was prepared to suffer. You should prepared to emulate his example by remaining equally loyal to it.'

Although the story of the marriage of the Frankish princess Ingund to the Spanish Visigoth prince Hermangild dates from the end rather than the beginning of the sixth century it helpfully illustrates the concerns that seem to lie behind the writing of the Athanasian Creed.

According to Gregory of Tours in his *History of the Franks*, when Ingund arrived in Spain:

> Her stepmother-in-law Goiswinth received her very warmly, but it was soon apparent that she had no intention of allowing her to remain a Catholic. She talked

---

[41] Kelly, *The Athanasian Creed*, 78.

> with her in a kindly way, and tried to persuade her to be re-baptized in the Arian heresy. Ingund had the courage to refuse. 'It is enough for me that I have been cleansed once for all from original sin by a baptism that will save my soul, and that I have made clear my belief in the Holy Trinity one and indivisible,' she said. 'I hereby confirm that I believe this with all my heart and that I will never go back on this article of faith.' When she heard this the Queen lost her temper completely. She seized the girl by the hair and threw her to the ground: then she kicked her until she was covered with blood, had her stripped naked and ordered her to be thrown into the baptismal pool. There are many witnesses who can tell how Ingund refused to budge an inch from the faith which we share.[42]

Gregory then goes on say that not only did Ingund refuse to become an Arian, but she also:

> ... began to persuade her husband to give up his belief in the false Arian heresy and to accept instead the true Catholic faith. For a long time he resisted, but in the end he was persuaded by her arguments and converted to the Catholic religion. He was anointed with chrism and took the name John.[43]

The best explanation as to why the Creed was written would seem to be that it was written for the sake of people like Ingund, to strengthen and equip them to remain firm in their faith 'in the Holy Trinity, one and indivisible' and to share that faith with those around them.

If we ask why the Christological section was included if the pressing issue was remaining faithful in the face of the Arian assault on the Trinity, there are two answers.

First, as previously explained, the author of the Creed seems to have been following on after an established bipartite creedal pattern which involved a section on Christology following after a section on the Trinity.

---

[42] Gregory of Tours, *The History of the Franks*, vol. 38 (London: Penguin, 1974), 302.
[43] Gregory of Tours, *The History of the Franks*, 302.

Secondly, and probably more importantly, the history of the fifth century seems to have shown the author of the Creed that rejecting the Arian denial of the full deity of the Son and the Holy Spirit was not sufficient to safeguard orthodox biblical teaching. Some of those who opposed Arianism then departed from orthodoxy by holding either that the incarnate Son was less than fully human (the Apollinarian heresy) or that there were two persons, one divine and one human, co-existing alongside one another (the Nestorian heresy). As noted above, the controversy about such departures from the Catholic faith seems to have died down by the time the Creed was written, and it was not such an important threat as Visigothic Arianism, but the author of the Creed obviously felt that the danger of people departing from the faith in this area was still a real one and that appropriate warning and instruction was therefore called for.

How the Athanasian Creed Came to Be Used across the Western Church

The Sixth Century

Although most scholars see Caesarius' collection of homilies as the earliest testimony to the existence of the Athanasian Creed, there is another possible echo of it from early in the sixth century. This is in the work of a man called Avitus who was Bishop of Vienne in south eastern Gaul from 490–519 and another champion of Catholic orthodoxy against Arianism.

In some fragments from a work on the divinity of the Holy Spirit he writes that 'we read' of the Holy Spirit 'as neither made, nor begotten, nor created,' that 'We declare the Holy Spirit to proceed from the Son and the Father' and that 'the Catholic faith' teaches that 'it belongs to the Holy Spirit to proceed from the Father and the Son.'[44] These could possibly be echoes of verse 23 of the Athanasian Creed, with 'we read' referring to the Creed. However, the teaching in these quotations had become widely accepted among Catholic theologians since the time of Augustine and there is not a close verbal similarity to what is said in the Creed. The idea that Avitus is echoing the Creed, although possible, is therefore not probable.

---

[44] Quotations in Kelly, *The Athanasian Creed*, 38.

There is greater probability that there is an echo of the Creed in the confession of faith made by the Visigothic King Recared of Toledo at the Third Council of Toledo in 589, in which he formally renounced Arianism in favour of Catholicism. This confession of faith draws on two fifth-century creedal statements, *The Faith of Damasus* and the *Little Writing in the Form of Creed* attributed to Bishop Pastor of Palencia, and two passages have also been seen as echoing the Athanasian Creed.

The passages in question run as follows:

> ... so that the Father who has begotten is one person, the Son who is begotten is another, but both subsist in the Godhead of one substance. The Father from whom the Son is derived is himself from none other

> ... but just as it is an evidence of true salvation to perceive the Trinity in the unity, and the unity in the Trinity ...[45]

Here there do seem to be verbal echoes of verses 5, 21 and 3 of the Athanasian Creed and the likelihood that this is the case is increased by the fact that we know that Recared's confession draws on the two other existing creedal statements mentioned above. Whoever wrote the confession for Recared drew on existing creedal material and seems to have also made use of the Athanasian Creed for this purpose.

The Seventh Century

Moving on to the seventh century, we find use being made of several passages from the Athanasian Creed in the statement of faith issued by the Fourth Council of Toledo in 633. For example:

> ... proclaiming the unity in the Godhead we neither confuse the persons nor divide the substance. We declare the Father to be made of none nor begotten; the Son we affirm to be not made by the Father but begotten; the Holy Spirit we profess to be neither created nor begotten, but proceeding from the Father and the Son

This draws on verses 3–4 and 21–23 of the Creed and its declaration that Christ is 'equal to the Father in respect of his divinity, less than the Father

---

[45] Quotations in Kelly, *The Athanasian Creed*, 38.

in respect of his humanity' draws on verse 33.[46] In all there are five passages in the statement of faith that draw on sections of the Athanasian Creed and the use made of these passages indicates that by the beginning of the seventh century the Creed had become known and accepted as an orthodox statement of faith which later statements could rightly build on.

Further evidence of the acceptance of the authority of the Creed in the seventh century is provided by the Church council held at Autun in Burgundy in about 670. The first canon of this council laid down that; 'If any Presbyter, Deacon, Subdeacon, or Clerk, doth not unreprovably recite the Creed which the Apostles delivered by the inspiration of the Holy Ghost, and also The Faith of the Holy Prelate Athanasius, let him be censured by the bishop.'[47]

The two statements of faith referred to here are the Apostles' Creed (which was believed to have been directly given to the Apostles by the Spirit on the day of Pentecost) and the Athanasian Creed. In this canon, as in the Caesarian homily collection, the Athanasian Creed is seen as a tool for the instruction of the clergy (subdeacons and clerks being viewed as lesser ranks of holy orders) and the reason they are required to recite it is a proof of both their knowledge and their orthodoxy.

The Eighth and Ninth Centuries

In the eighth and ninth centuries there is increasing evidence for the knowledge and use of the Athanasian Creed in the orbit of the Carolingian dynasty which ruled over Gaul and much of the rest of what is now Western Europe.

- There are the earliest manuscripts containing the original text of the Creed (as opposed to the edited version in the *Zwiefalten Codex*);
- Commentaries on the Creed begin to make their appearance, the earliest, the Fortunatus Commentary,[48] being generally dated to the end of the eighth century although it could possibly be earlier;[49]

---

[46] Quotations in Kelly, *The Athanasian Creed*, 38.
[47] Quotation in Waterland, *A Critical History*, 16.
[48] For this commentary see Waterland, *A Critical History*, 171–80.
[49] For discussion of the commentaries see G. W. D. Ommanney, *A Critical Dissertation on the Athanasian Creed* (Oxford: OUP, 1897), Ch. IV.

- There is evidence that the Creed continued to be used as a means of training the clergy. Thus a canon of a synod held at Rheims in 852 required the clergy 'to memorize the creed, grasp its meaning and be able to expound it in the popular speech;'[50]
- There are Psalters dating from second half of the eight century onwards in which the Creed is bound up with other additional texts such as the Canticles, the Lord's Prayer and the Apostles' Creed;
- There is evidence for the Creed beginning to be included in the liturgy and sung as a canticle. Thus Haito, Bishop of Basle from 807–823, laid down in his *Capitula ecclesiastica* that priests should learn the Creed by heart and recite it during the 6am office of Prime every Sunday.

The end of the eight century also saw the first evidence for the use of the Athanasian Creed in England. In about 798 Denebert, the bishop-elect of Worcester cited verses 1, 3–6, 20–22 and 24–25 as a token of his orthodoxy prior to his consecration by Ethelbert, the Archbishop of Canterbury.

The Middle Ages

During the Middle Ages the Athanasian Creed, which was, as we have said, regarded as the work of Athanasius himself, continued to be used for the instruction of the clergy.

It also continued to be used regularly in the liturgy and in circles associated with the Cluniac monastic reform movement its use was extended so that it was recited at Prime not only on Sundays, but on every day of the week from Christmas to Epiphany and Easter to Whitsun. This practice is also found in the collection of English medieval liturgical texts known as the *Sarum Rite*.

Because of its use in the liturgy it came to be classified with the other two creeds that were similarly used, the Apostles and Nicene Creeds, and so by the thirteenth century it became customary to refer to the 'three creeds' (in Latin *tria symbola* or *triplex symbolum*).

---

[50] Kelly, *The Athanasian Creed*, 42.

The Reformation

At the Reformation the Roman Catholic Church continued to regard the Athanasian Creed as theologically authoritative and in his reform of Roman Catholic liturgical usage in 1568 Pope Pius V maintained the practice of its recitation at Prime every Sunday.

On the Protestant side the Lutheran tradition included the Athanasian Creed in the *Book of Concord* of 1580 alongside the Apostles' and Nicene Creeds as one of 'The three ecumenical or universal creeds.'[51] The Reformed tradition meanwhile recognised it as authoritative in Huldrych Zwingli's 1531 *Exposition of the Faith*, in the *Gallican Confession* of 1559, in the *Belgic Confession* of 1566 and in the Canons of the Synod of Dort in 1619. Article 5 of the *Gallican Confession*, for instance, declares: 'we confess the three creeds, to wit: the Apostles', the Nicene, and the Athanasian, because they are in accordance with the Word of God.'[52]

As was noted in the introduction, the reformed Church of England also continued to uphold the authority of the Athanasian Creed and made provision for its regular liturgical use. Like the *Gallican Confession*, Article VIII of the Thirty Nine Articles bases the authority of the Athanasian Creed on its conformity with Scripture and, as we saw, with the abolition of the office of Prime, the Church of England transferred the recitation of the Creed to the office of Morning Prayer on thirteen days a year. On the one hand, this liturgical change was a reduction of the number of times the Creed should be recited. However, on the other hand, the provision for it to be recited by 'by the Minister and people' meant that its recitation was no longer the preserve of monks, or the clergy, but was something in which the whole people of God, clergy and laity, were to be involved together.

Developments in the Church of England Since the Reformation

From the end of the seventeenth century onwards, as part of a wider movement away from traditional Christian orthodoxy, appreciation and use of the Athanasian Creed has been in decline across the Western

---

[51] See the *Book of Concord* at http://bookofconcord.org/creeds.php
[52] *Gallican Confession*, Article 5 at https://cfcreforme.blogspot.com/2007/11/gallican-confession-of-faith-1559.html (Accessed 8 April 2019).

Church. As noted in the Introduction, this has also been true in the case of the Church of England.

The Seventeenth and Eighteenth Centuries

The first major sign of this movement in the Church of England came in 1689 when a Church of England commission tasked with considering how the Church of England could be more welcoming to Protestant dissenters proposed addressing objections to the damnatory clauses in the Athanasian Creed by adding a rubric to the *Book of Common Prayer* explaining that these clauses 'are to be understood as relating only to those, who obstinately deny the substance of the Christian faith.'[53]

This proposal met with strong opposition in the Lower House of Convocation (the meeting of the representatives of the clergy of the Church of England) and therefore got nowhere. However, opposition to the Athanasian Creed continued, not only among those who objected to what they saw as the unnecessary harshness of the damnatory clauses, but also among those who embraced an Arian or Deist form of theology and who therefore objected to the theology of the Creed as a whole.

This continuing opposition was countered by Waterland in his 1724 work *A Critical History of the Athanasian Creed* to which we have already referred. In 1712 a Church of England Clergyman named Samuel Clarke, who took an Arian view of God, published a book entitled *The Scripture Doctrine of The Trinity* in which he set out a series of reasons why The Church of England should either abandon the Athanasian Creed completely, or at least not impose its acceptance and use in the *Articles* and the *Book of Common Prayer*.[54]

Holding that the reasons put forward by Clarke were the strongest the opponents of the Creed had to offer ('the closest and strongest that can be offered on that side'),[55] Waterland subjected them to critical scrutiny and explained why they were not persuasive and why therefore the Church of England was 'vindicated, both as to the receiving and retaining, the

---

[53] Quoted in George Miller, *Observations on the Doctrines of Christianity, in Reference to Arianism, Illustrating the Moderation of the Established Church* (London: Rivington, 1825), 163–164.
[54] Samuel Clarke, *The Scripture Doctrine of the Trinity* (London: James Knapton, 1712), 446–454.
[55] Waterland, *A Critical History*, 150.

Athanasian Creed.'⁵⁶ His overall conclusion was that the Creed would still be needed in the Church as a safeguard against heresy so long as the doctrines it contained continued to come under attack:

> Upon the whole, I look upon it as exceedingly useful, and even necessary, for every Church to have some such form as this, or something equivalent, open and common to all its members; that none may be led astray for want of proper caution, and previous instruction in what so nearly concerns the whole structure and fabric of the Christian faith. As to this particular form, it has so long prevailed, and has so well answered to the use intended, that, all things considered, there can be no sufficient reason for changing any part of it, much less for laying the whole aside. There are several other Creeds, very good ones (though somewhat larger) which had they been made choice of for common use, might possibly have done as well. The Creeds I mean (of which there is a great number) drawn up after the Council of Chalcedon and purposely contrived to obviate all the heresies that ever had infested the Christian Church. But, those that dislike this Creed, would much more dislike the other; being still more particular, and explicit in regard to the Nestorian, Eutychian, and Monothelite heresies, and equally full and clear for the doctrine of the Trinity.
>
> To conclude; so long as there shall be any men left to oppose the doctrines which this creed contains, so long will it be expedient, and even necessary to continue the use of it, in order to preserve the rest: And, I suppose, when we have none remaining to find fault with the doctrines, there will be none to object against the use of the creed, or so much as to wish to have it set aside.⁵⁷

Waterland's vast knowledge of the history, use, and interpretation of the Creed, and the force and clarity of his arguments, meant that his work

---

⁵⁶ Waterland, *A Critical History*, 150.
⁵⁷ Waterland, *A Critical History*, 162.

came to be regarded as the definitive Anglican defence of the Creed and the proposal to abolish the use of the Creed in the Church of England, or to make its use no longer obligatory, came to nothing. In the Church of England the position of the Creed in the Articles and the Prayer Book remained unchanged throughout the eighteenth century.

By contrast, the newly formed Episcopal Church in the United States decided to remove the Creed from its versions of the Articles and the Prayer Book at its third General Convention in 1789.

The Nineteenth Century

However, the fact that the position of the Athanasian Creed within the Church of England remained unchanged did not mean that opposition to it simply vanished. The issues about the Creed that had surfaced at the end of the seventeenth century still remained and they re-emerged in the widespread debate about the Creed that took place in the Church of England from 1870 onwards.

In 1867, the government of Lord Derby had established a Royal Commission on ritual with the brief to investigate 'the rubrics, orders, and directions for regulating the course and conduct of public worship.'[58] In their fourth report, published in 1870, the members of the Commission recommended retaining the rubric in the Book of Common Prayer governing the use of the Athanasian Creed. Nevertheless, like their predecessors in 1689, they also recommended that an explanatory note about the damnatory clauses should be added explaining 'that the condemnations in this Confession of Faith are to be no otherwise understood than as a solemn warning of the peril of those who wilfully reject the Catholic Faith.'[59]

Having produced the report, seventeen of the twenty-seven members then dissented from its conclusions in a lengthy appendix. However, while they agreed in dissenting from the report's conclusions, they did not agree about an alternative way forward. A lay Evangelical dissentient,

---

[58] Quoted in Joshua Bennett, 'The Age of Athanasius, The Church of England and the Athanasian Creed 1870–1873,' *Church History and Religious Culture*, 97 (2017): 227.

[59] Quoted in Bennett, 'The Age of Athanasius,' 228.

Joseph Napier, suggested that the report had exceeded its powers in proposing a particular interpretation of the Creed, while others, such as the Bishop of Bristol and Gloucester, Charles Ellicott, the Dean of Westminster, Arthur Stanley, and the new Archbishop of Canterbury, Archibald Tait, suggested that the damnatory clauses should be removed, or that the use of the Creed should be made optional, or that it should cease to be used in public worship.

Various reasons were suggested by the dissentients and their subsequent supporters as to why the Church's use of the Creed needed to change. Mostly frequently it was argued that:

> ... the creed's damnatory clauses circumscribed God's mercy, and effected an unchristian elevation of precisionist theology over ethics and Christian charity which unjustifiably narrowed the ends and breadth of Christ's church.[60]

In other words, the Creed unduly limited both God and the Church.

However, it was also argued that the Athanasian Creed was in fact a hymn or psalm rather than a creedal document and that it had been imposed on the Church in the name of Athanasius in an act of 'medieval imposture' and Stanley further suggested that the Creed lacked proper 'humility and hesitancy' in insisting on the acceptance of an exact phraseology concerning the relations between the persons of the Trinity.[61]

The arguments of the dissentients produced a 'torrent of denunciatory sermons, pamphlets, and public letters' with the Oxford high church leader H P Liddon going as far as to tell Archbishop Tait that he would resign from the ministry were the status of the Creed to be altered or downgraded.[62] As Joshua Bennett writes in his account of the controversy, those opposed to change:

---

[60] Bennett, 'The Age of Athanasius,' 229.
[61] A. P. Stanley, 'The Athanasian Creed,' *Contemporary Review*, 15 (1870): 139, 157.
[62] Bennett, 'The Age of Athanasius,' 238.

> ... saw all attempts to modify or rescind the creed as a capitulation to advanced dissent and even outright agnosticism by those one pamphleteer labelled as the 'Erastian or Broad Church party,' and another as 'the Rationalists.'[63]

In their view, those opposed to the Creed were the lineal descendants of the Socinians, the anti-Trinitarian heretics of the sixteenth and seventeenth centuries.[64]

Unlike in Ireland, where the Synod of the newly disestablished Church of Ireland voted in 1876 to delete the rubric enjoining the use of the Creed from the Prayer book, in England the opponents of any change to the Creed's text or status won the day.

On 26 April 1872 the members of the Lower House of Convocation followed the example of their predecessors in 1689 by decisively passing a motion holding that the Church should continue to retain the use of the Creed without any alteration to its text.[65] In May the following year the Upper and Lower Houses of Convocation then produced a joint synodical declaration which ran as follows:

> For the removal of doubts and to prevent disquietude in the use of the creed commonly called the Creed of St. Athanasius, this synod doth solemnly declare:
>
> 1. That the confession of our Christian faith, commonly called the Creed of St. Athanasius, doth not make any addition to the faith as contained in the Holy Scripture, but warneth against errors which from time to time have arisen in the Church of Christ.

---

[63] Bennett, 'The Age of Athanasius,' 238.
[64] The bulk of the opposition came from High Church Anglicans. The majority Evangelical position, as reflected in the Evangelical newspaper the *Record*, became that the text of the Creed should be unaltered, but that its use should be made optional on the grounds that this would avoid unnecessary conflict between Anglicans and Non-Conformists over a non-biblical document (Bennett, 'The Age of Athanasius,' 234–235).
[65] *Chronicle of Convocation*, 26 Apr. 1872, 422–458.

2. That as Holy Scripture in divers places doth promise life to them that believe and declare the condemnation of them that believe not, so doth the Church in this confession declare the necessity for all who would be in a state of salvation of holding fast the Catholic faith, and the great peril of rejecting the same. Wherefore the warnings in this confession of faith are to be understood no otherwise than the like warnings in Holy Scripture, for we must receive God's threatenings even as His promises, in such wise as they are generally set forth in Holy Writ.[66] Moreover, the Church doth not herein pronounce judgment on any particular person or persons, God alone being the judge of all.[67]

The Twentieth Century

The decisions made in 1872 and 1873 have remained unaltered. The Church of England has not since then sought to change the use of the *Athanasian Creed* as this is laid down in the *Book of Common Prayer*, nor has it issued any new statement about the nature of the Creed and how its damnatory clauses should be understood.

However, during the course of the twentieth century there was a radical, though unofficial, change in the status of the Creed in the Church of England. As explained in the introduction, it became the neglected creed, the creed that was increasingly simply not used in the Church's public worship.

In the absence of any detailed research on the topic we cannot say precisely why this change took place. However, six reasons seem likely.

- First, during this period any notion of eternal damnation became increasingly contested and for this reason the damnatory clauses will have continued to be a stumbling block preventing people from accepting or using the Creed.

- Secondly, in a period in which there was continuing debate about adhering to the Trinitarian and Christological teaching of the

---

[66] An allusion to the words of Article XVII of the *Thirty Nine Articles*.
[67] *Chronicle of Convocation*, 9 May 1873, 405–406.

Patristic period, the Creed's uncompromising insistence on this teaching will likewise have been a stumbling block.

- Thirdly, during this period there was increasing emphasis on the importance of Christian social and political action rather than on 'abstract theology' and so for many people the Creed may simply have been seen as irrelevant.

- Fourthly, during this period there was an increasing emphasis on the importance of ecumenism and the Apostles and Nicene Creeds, rather than the Athanasian Creed, came to be seen as the two key ecumenical statements of faith which the churches should employ.[68]

- Fifthly, during this period there was an increasing emphasis on the importance of using forms of liturgy that would appeal to an increasingly secular population, unaccustomed to taking part in regular public worship, and the length and complexity of the Athanasian Creed meant that it would not fit easily into these more 'user friendly' forms of service.

- Sixthly, there seems to be no record of any attempt to impose discipline on those who did not observe the rubric in the *Book of Common Prayer* concerning the use of the Creed. This being the case, there was no incentive on anybody who was wavering on the matter to use the Creed because there would be no consequences if they did not.

Neglect of the Athanasian Creed was also both reflected and encouraged by the liturgical revision which took place in the Church of England during the twentieth century. The proposed 1928 version of the Prayer Book provided a new translation of the Creed and noted more occasions when the creed might be used than those set down in the *Book of Common Prayer*. However, 'it made its recitation entirely optional, on certain days allowed the Trinitarian or Christological section alone to be

---

[68] It is noteworthy in this context that the Church of England's ecumenical agreements have mentioned agreement with other churches over the use of the Apostles' and Nicene Creeds, but have ignored the Athanasian Creed.

said, and stipulated that when the new translation provided was employed the so-called damnatory clauses might be omitted.'[69]

The modern language services known as *Series 1, 2 and 3* published between 1965 and 1972 made no provision at all for the use of the Creed and the same was true of the services of the *Alternative Service Book* of 1980. These modern language forms of liturgy came to replace the *Book of Common Prayer* as the normal basis for public worship in the Church of England and this meant that the Athanasian Creed largely vanished from such worship.

As noted in the introduction, *Common Worship*, which began to come into use from 2000 onwards allows for the optional use of the Creed. However, although it contains a modern paraphrase of the Christological section of the Creed[70] it does not have a modern English translation of the Creed as a whole in the same way that it has modern English translations of the Apostles' and Nicene Creeds.

The Anglican Communion

The situation in the Anglican Communion has been similar to that in the Church of England. The use of the Athanasian Creed has never been officially abolished, but it has become largely neglected.

Resolution 30 of the 1908 Lambeth Conference of Anglican Bishops is the only authoritative statement on this issue by the Communion as whole. It states that the decision whether or not to use the Creed is one for the individual churches of the Communion to make.

> The Conference, having had under consideration the liturgical use of the *Quicunque Vult*, expresses its opinion that, inasmuch as the use or disuse of this hymn is not a term of communion, the several Churches of the Anglican Communion may rightly decide for themselves what in their varying circumstances is desirable; but the Conference urges that, if any change of rule or usage is

---

[69] Kelly, *The Athanasian Creed*, 50.
[70] Section E7 of 'Creeds and Alternative Affirmations of Faith.'

made, full regard should be had to the maintenance of the Catholic faith in its integrity, to the commendation of that faith to the minds of men, and to the relief of disquieted consciences.[71]

The decision that the churches of the Anglican Communion have increasingly made is not to use the Creed and this is reflected in the way in which the official guide to *The Principles of Canon Law Common to the Churches of the Anglican Communion* published in 2008 mentions the Apostles' and Nicene Creeds as sources of Anglican doctrine, but says nothing about the Athanasian Creed.[72]

Interestingly, however, there has recently been a re-assertion of the importance of the Athanasian Creed by some Anglicans as part of the renewal of orthodox Anglicanism that has taken place since the Lambeth Conference of 1998.

Thus Article 3 of the *Jerusalem Declaration* issued by the Global Anglican Futures conference (GAFCON) states: 'We uphold the four Ecumenical Councils and the three historic Creeds as expressing the rule of faith of the one holy catholic and apostolic church.'[73] In this statement the four ecumenical councils are the Councils of Nicaea (325), First Constantinople (381), Ephesus (431) and Chalcedon (451) and the 'three historic creeds' are the Apostles', Nicene and Athanasian Creeds.

Thus also, Article 4 of the Theological Statement of the Anglican Church in North America (ACNA) reverses the traditional neglect of the Athanasian Creed by the Episcopal Church and declares:

> We confess as proved by most certain warrants of Holy Scripture the historic faith of the undivided church as

---

[71] Roger Coleman, ed., *Resolutions of the Lambeth Conferences, 1867–1988* (Toronto: Anglican Book Centre, 1992), 33.
[72] *The Principles of Canon Law Common to the Churches of the Anglican Communion* (London: The Anglican Communion Office, 2008), 58.
[73] Text at https://www.gafcon.org/resources/the-complete-jerusalem-statement (Accessed 8 April 2019).

declared in the three Catholic Creeds: the Apostles', the Nicene, and the Athanasian.[74]

In similar fashion Questions 22–24 of the new ACNA catechism *To Be a Christian* run as follows:

> 22. Which Creeds does the Church acknowledge?
>
> The Church acknowledges the Apostles' Creed, the Nicene Creed, and the Athanasian Creed. (Articles of Religion, 8)
>
> 23. Why do you acknowledge these Creeds?
>
> I acknowledge these Creeds with the Church because they are grounded in Holy Scripture and are faithful expressions of its teaching. (1 Corinthians 15:3–11; Philippians 2:6–11)
>
> 24. Why should you know these Creeds?
>
> I should know these Creeds because they state the essential beliefs of the Christian faith.[75]

The Athanasian Creed in the Eastern Church

Although the Athanasian Creed originated in the Western Church, it seems to have become known to people in the Eastern Church from the ninth century onwards.

- In 808 Frankish Monks who lived on the Mount of Olives in Jerusalem were charged with heresy for holding that the Holy Spirit proceeds from the Father and the Son (the so called 'double procession') rather than from the Father alone and they appealed to the Athanasian Creed in support of the orthodoxy of their position.
- Cardinal Humbert of Silva Candida included three extracts from the Athanasian Creed in a treatise on the procession of the Holy Spirit which he addressed to the Byzantine Emperor Constantine XI in 1054.

---

[74] Text at http://www.anglicanchurch.net/index.php/main/Theology/ (Accessed 8 April 2019).
[75] The text of *To Be a Christian* can be found at http://anglicanchurch.net/?/main/catechism (Accessed 8 April, 2019).

- Hugh Etherian, a Western theologian who held an important place at the court of the Byzantine Emperor Manuel I, gave a prominent place to verse 23 of the Athanasian Creed in a dossier of authorities supporting the Western belief in the double procession of the Holy Spirit which he assembled in 1176.
- Envoys from Pope Gregory IX appealed to the authority of the Athanasian Creed in a conference with representatives of the Eastern Church held at Nympha in 1254.
- In 1252 Cistercian monks visiting Nicaea saw what they described as an 'ancient' Greek copy of the text, an event which points to the Athanasian Creed in its entirety being available in Greek in the East from a least the end of the twelfth century.
- John Beccus, the pro-Western Patriarch of Constantinople (1275-82), quoted verse 23 in Greek in a collection of material from the Fathers supporting the double procession.

Although Eastern theologians originally rejected the Athanasian authorship of the Creed, at the end of the fourteenth and the beginning of the fifteenth centuries Eastern theologians came to hold that the Creed was indeed the work of Athanasius, but that the clause supporting the double procession was a later Western addition. On that basis the Creed became accepted as a theological authority, but unlike in the West it was never used in the liturgy.

The Eastern position changed again in the nineteenth century when acquaintance with the rejection of Athanasian authorship by Western scholars led Eastern writers to deny once more that it was written by Athanasius and to denounce it as a Western fabrication designed to provide support for the double procession.

Today Eastern Orthodox theologians would see the Athanasian Creed as an historic expression of the Western theological tradition which they would not regard as theologically authoritative and which they would disagree with over the issue of the double procession.[76]

---

[76] See Kelly, *The Athanasian Creed*, 44–48 for details of the knowledge and reception of the Athanasian Creed in the Eastern Church.

3. The Theology of the Athanasian Creed

The Importance of Holding Fast to the Catholic Faith (verses 1–2)

¹Whosoever will be saved: before all things it is necessary that he hold the Catholick Faith. ²Which Faith except every one do keep whole and undefiled: without doubt he shall perish everlastingly.

What these verses mean by the 'Catholic faith' is the corpus of authoritative teaching handed down to the Church by the Apostles in fulfilment of the commission given to them by Jesus to be witnesses to who he was and what he taught (Matthew 28:20, Acts 1:8).

The New Testament testifies to the existence of this authoritative teaching in a number of places. Thus Acts 2:42 describes the first Christians as devoting themselves to 'the apostles' teaching,' Romans 6:17 talks about 'the standard of teaching to which you were committed' and Jude 3 refers to 'the faith which was once for all delivered to the saints.'

It is this authoritative teaching, expounded in the New Testament, and handed down in the Church by a succession of faithful leaders and teachers, which the Athanasian Creed declares people need to hold fast to in order to be saved from eternal damnation.

As the 1873 synodical declaration indicated, the theological basis for this declaration is the New Testament teaching that belief brings salvation whereas failure to believe brings condemnation. Mark 16:16 states 'He who believes and is baptised will be saved; but he who does not believe will be condemned.'[77] In similar fashion, we are told in John 3:16–18 'For God so loved the world that he gave his only Son, that whoever believes in him should not perish but have eternal life. For God sent his Son into the world, not to condemn the world, but that the world might be saved

---

[77] Mark 16:9–20 are generally regarded today as an addition to the original text of Mark and therefore as non- Canonical. However, in the history of the Church they have been regarded as the original ending of Mark and this historic position can still be defended. See for example J. W. Burgon, *The Last Twelve Verses of the Gospel According to S. Mark* (Oxford: OUP, 1871) and W. R. Farmer, *The Last Twelve Verses of Mark* (Cambridge: CUP, 1974).

through him. He who believes in him is not condemned; he who does not believe is condemned already, because he has not believed in the name of the only Son of God.' For these verses, and for the New Testament as a whole, belief is the thing that is of primary significance (necessary 'before all things' as the Creed puts it) because, although belief has to express itself in a changed pattern of behaviour, it is belief that places us in a state of salvation. As Romans 3:28 puts it, 'we are justified (i.e. have a right relationship with God) by faith.'

The link between what is said in these verses from the New Testament and what is taught in the opening verses of the Athanasian Creed lies in the fact that belief in Jesus leading to salvation means belief in the teaching of the Apostles. Because Christ has ascended to the right hand of the Father, he no longer presents himself directly to us as the object of our belief as was the case during the years of his earthly ministry. Instead he is presented to us in the form of the teaching of the Apostles. As Paul says, the Apostles are the 'ambassadors' of Christ (2 Corinthians 5:20) appointed by him to speak and act on his behalf. This means that our belief or unbelief in the Apostles' teaching is our belief or unbelief in Christ himself.

As we have noted, the 'Catholic faith' to which the Athanasian Creed refers is the teaching of the Apostles as this is expounded in the New Testament and has been handed down in the Church. It follows that belief or unbelief in the Catholic faith is also belief or unbelief in Christ and that if we wish to be saved rather than condemned we must believe what the Catholic faith teaches. Furthermore, we have to go on believing it even when, like Catholics in Gaul and Spain in the fifth and sixth centuries, we face pressure to do otherwise. As the parable of the sower (Mark 4:1–20) makes clear, it is persistence in the faith that brings salvation.

We must also go on believing the faith in its entirety, 'whole and undefiled' as the Athanasian Creed puts it. This is because we cannot legitimately choose to believe some bits of the faith and reject others. It is the Catholic faith as a whole that has been presented to us to be the object of our belief and if we decide not to believe parts of it then we enter into a state of unbelief and therefore become subject to condemnation.

When the Creed says that the person who fails to keep the faith will 'without doubt' perish everlastingly, what it has in view is someone who persists in a state of unbelief. It does not rule out the possibility that someone who is currently in a state of unbelief may repent and be forgiven and therefore be saved. What it does do is warn that unbelief is an ultimately serious matter because if we persist in it eternal loss will be the result.

Finally, we need to heed the implicit warning in the 1873 declaration against seeking to pronounce that any particular individual is in fact subject to the condemnation referred to in the Creed. It is God's prerogative to make that judgement and not ours.

The Catholic Faith in the Trinity (verses 3–6)

³And the Catholick Faith is this: That we worship one God in Trinity, and Trinity in Unity; ⁴Neither confounding the Persons: nor dividing the Substance. ⁵For there is one Person of the Father, another of the Son: and another of the Holy Ghost. ⁶But the Godhead of the Father, of the Son, and of the Holy Ghost, is all one: the Glory equal, the Majesty co-eternal.

Having said how important it is to hold the Catholic faith, the Athanasian Creed next goes on to summarise the Catholic faith in the Tri-unity of God.

As W H Griffith Thomas explains in his book *The Principles of Theology*, the apostolic teaching contained in the New Testament contains two lines of teaching about God.

> (a) One line of teaching insists on the unity of the Godhead (1 Cor. 8:4; Jas. 2:19); and (b) the other reveals distinctions within the Godhead (Matt. 3:16, 17; 28:19, 2 Cor. 13:14). We see clearly that (1) the Father is God (Matt. 11:25; Rom. 15:6; Eph. 4:6); (2) the Son is God (John 1:1, 18; 20:28; Acts 20:28; Rom. 9:5; Heb. 1:8; Col. 2:9; Phil. 2:6; 2 Peter 1:1); (3) the Holy Spirit is God (Acts 5:3, 4; 1 Cor. 2:10, 11; Eph. 2:22); (4) the Father, Son and Holy Spirit are distinct from one another, sending and being sent, honouring and being honoured. The Father honours the Son, the Son honours the Father, and the Holy Spirit honours the Son (John 15:26; 16:13, 14; 17:1, 8, 18, 23). (5) Nevertheless, whatever relations of subordination there may be between the Persons in the

working out of redemption, the Three are alike regarded as God.[78]

Augustine makes the same point about the dual nature of the New Testament witness when he says to God in Book XV of his work *On the Trinity*:

> O Lord our God, we believe in Thee, the Father and the Son and the Holy Spirit. For the Truth would not say, Go, baptise all nations in the name of the Father and of the Son and of the Holy Spirit, unless thou wast a Trinity. Nor wouldest thou, O Lord God, bid us to be baptized in the name of Him who is not the Lord God. Nor would the divine voice have said, Hear, O Israel, the Lord thy God is one God, unless thou wert so a Trinity as to be one Lord God. And if thou, O God, wert thyself the Father, and wert thyself the Son, Thy Word Jesus Christ, and the Holy Spirit your gift, we should not read in the book of truth, 'God sent his Son;' nor wouldst Thou, O Only-begotten, say of the Holy Spirit, 'Whom the Father will send in my name;' and 'Whom I will send to you from the Father.'[79]

Verses 3–4 of The Athanasian Creed reflects this dual New Testament witness by explaining that the Catholic faith involves Christians worshipping 'one God in Trinity, and Trinity in Unity; Neither confounding the Persons: nor dividing the Substance.'

The first clause here affirms the positive truth that the Catholic faith teaches us to worship the one God as the Father, Son and the Holy Spirit, three persons who are eternally distinct, yet eternally united by reason of the one divine nature which they all possess.

The second clause rejects two errors which existed during the Patristic period and which are incompatible with holding the Catholic faith in the distinction of persons and unity of nature in God.

---

[78] W. H. Griffith Thomas, *The Principles of Theology* (London: Church Book Room Press, 1951), 24.

[79] Augustine, *On the Trinity* XV:28 in *The Nicene & Post Nicene Fathers* Vol III (Edinburgh and Grand Rapids: T&T Clark/Eerdmans 1998), 227.

The first is the error of 'confounding the persons.' As J Hamer Rawdon writes in his commentary on the Creed, this term is used to 'describe the doctrine of several false teachers, who lived from the close of the second century to the middle of the third century.' This doctrine 'is generally called Sabellianism, from one of them, whose name was Sabellius.'[80]

These false teachers, he says

> ... in their professed desire to uphold the unity of the Divine Nature, virtually denied the existence in it of three Persons, speaking of the Father, the Son and the Holy Ghost, as if they were but three *ways* in which God had revealed Himself to man, or three *characters*, which he had assumed, or again, three *influences*, or *extensions* of the Divine Nature, so that the Father might be at one time the Son, at another the Holy Ghost, while some of them even held, or were believed to have held, that the Father suffered on the cross; and others taught that the Son and the Holy Ghost, when they had accomplished the work for which they had come forth from the Father, would return into, and be eventually so merged in Him, as to lose their personality.[81]

The second is the error of 'dividing the substance.' To quote Rawdon again, this error was that 'of Arius who was condemned at the Council of Nice,[82] the First General Council, AD 325, and that of his followers the Seminarians (or half Arians) who were condemned at the Second General Council, that of Constantinople, AD 381.' This error consisted in 'making the Godhead – the divine nature or essence of the Son – to be different from that of the Father, inferior to it in fact, and making the Godhead, the divine nature of the Holy Ghost, to be different from, and inferior to, that of the Father and the Son.'[83]

---

[80] J. Hamer Rawdon, *The Athanasian Creed, Six Expository Addresses* (Collingwood: Trieste Publishing, 2017), 18.
[81] Rawdon, *The Athanasian Creed*, 18.
[82] More commonly known as the Council of Nicaea.
[83] Rawdon, *The Athanasian Creed*, 19–20.

As previously noted, this second error, which amounted to a form of tritheism, was that adhered to by the Visigoths at the time the Creed was written.

Verses 5–6 go on to explain why it is wrong for someone who wants to hold the Catholic faith to either confound the persons or divide the substance.

Verse 5 says that the reason it is wrong to 'confound the persons' is because the Catholic faith teaches us that 'there is one Person of the Father, another of the Son: and another of the Holy Ghost.' Verse 6 says this does not however mean that we can 'divide the substance' because the Catholic faith also teaches us that 'the Godhead of the Father, of the Son, and of the Holy Ghost, is all one: the Glory equal, the Majesty co-eternal.' God possesses glory and majesty because of his divine nature and this divine nature or 'Godhead' is possessed identically by all three persons.

In line with the apostolic witness in the New Testament, holding the Catholic faith thus means holding that God is one (because there is one divine nature), but God is also three (because there are three distinct persons who possess this one divine nature). As the hymn by Gilbert Rorison puts it, God is 'Three in One and One in Three.'[84]

The Common Divine Attributes (verses 7–12)

7 Such as the Father is, such is the Son: and such is the Holy Ghost. 8 The Father uncreate, the Son uncreate: and the Holy Ghost uncreate. 9 The Father incomprehensible, the Son incomprehensible: and the Holy Ghost incomprehensible. 10 The Father eternal, the Son eternal: and the Holy Ghost eternal. 11 And yet they are not three eternals: but one eternal. 12 As also there are not three incomprehensibles, nor three uncreated: but one uncreated, and one incomprehensible.

In verses 7–12 the Creed gives three examples of what it means to say that there is a single divine nature possessed by all three persons of the Trinity. In line with the biblical witness it teaches that as the creator of all things

---

[84] Gilbert Rorison, 'Three in One, and One in Three,' at https://hymnary.org/text/three_in_one_and_one_in_three (Accessed 8 April 2019).

(Genesis 1:1–2:3, Psalm 104) God is himself uncreated. It then goes on to say as the creator God is not bound by space and time. He is therefore is present in all places (Psalm 139:7–12, Jeremiah 23:24) – which is what is meant by the word 'incomprehensible,' used in the old sense of that which cannot be placed within limits as a translation of the word *immensus* in the original Latin text – and he is eternal (Deuteronomy 33:27, Psalm 90:1–2).

Because the Father, Son and Holy Spirit all possess the divine nature all three are uncreated, omnipresent and eternal. However, this does not mean that each of them separately is uncreated, omnipotent and eternal. That would mean that there were three gods. Rather they have these attributes together as the one God who is Trinity.

The Common Divine Names (verses 13–20)

13 So likewise the Father is Almighty, the Son Almighty: and the Holy Ghost Almighty. 14 And yet they are not three Almighties: but one Almighty. 15 So the Father is God, the Son is God: and the Holy Ghost is God. 16 And yet they are not three Gods: but one God. 17 So likewise the Father is Lord, the Son Lord: and the Holy Ghost Lord. 18 And yet not three Lords: but one Lord. 19 For like as we are compelled by the Christian verity: to acknowledge every Person by himself to be God and Lord; 20 So are we forbidden by the Catholick Religion: to say there be three Gods, or three Lords.

Like the names used for human beings in the Bible, the names used for God express who God is. God is the Almighty (Genesis 17:1), he is God (Genesis 1:1) and he is the Lord (Exodus 3:14). If these names express who God is, and if the three persons of the Trinity are all God, it follows that the divine names are applicable to each of them. Hence these verses of the Creed say that 'Christian verity' (i.e. Christian truth) compels us to say that all three persons of the Trinity are the Almighty, God and Lord. To quote Rawdon again:

> ... the three great names by which God revealed himself to the patriarchs and prophets, and which are given to Him in Scripture sometimes separately, and sometimes in combination, are ascribed to each Person of the Holy Trinity. Each is Almighty, each is God and each is Lord;

> i.e. Jehovah, the name by which God revealed to Moses at the bush, the 'I Am' (the Self-Existent One).[85]

As Rawdon goes on to say, just as the previous set of verses declared that the divine attributes were possessed by the persons together as the one Triune God, so also these verses declare that the 'Catholick religion' (i.e. orthodox Christianity) teaches us to confess:

> ... that, though these three divine and awful names belong to each Person by Himself, yet they do not so belong to each as if there were three Almighties, or three Gods, or three Lords, but again as three Persons in one divine substance, nature, or Godhead.[86]

Once again, tri-theism is rejected and the divine unity is asserted.

Divine Simplicity

Underlying what is said in verses 7–20 of the Athanasian Creed lies the doctrine of divine simplicity. This doctrine, which goes back to the earliest days of the Church,[87] teaches that God is simple rather than compound. That is to say, God is not made up of lots of different parts that together make up God.

The reason for denying that this the case is the biblical teaching that God is the creator of heaven and earth and therefore his existence precedes everything else. 'Before the mountains were brought forth, or ever thou hadst formed the earth and the world, from everlasting to everlasting thou art God' (Psalm 90:2).

---

[85] Rawdon, *The Athanasian Creed*, 27. It has been suggested that the use of the terms 'almighty,' 'God' and 'Lord' in this section of the Creed go back to the reference in Revelation 1:8 to 'the Lord God ... the Almighty.' However, if Revelation was the source of these terms one would expect the order of the names given in Revelation to be followed whereas the order in the Creed is other way round.

[86] Rawdon, *The Athanasian Creed*, 27.

[87] For example, St Irenaeus wrote in the second century that God 'is a simple uncompounded Being, without diverse members, and altogether like and equal to himself.' *Against Heresies* Bk II.13.3 in *The Ante-Nicene Fathers*, vol. 1, (Edinburgh and Grand Rapids, T&T Clark/Eerdmans, 1996), 374.

As the Puritan theologian Stephen Charnock explains, if God precedes everything else, as Psalm 90 teaches us that he did, then he must necessarily be simple rather than compound:

> God is the most simple being; for that which is first in nature, having nothing beyond it, cannot by any means be thought to be compounded; for whatsoever is so, depends upon the parts whereof it is compounded, and so is not the first being.[88]

The point that Charnock is making here is that that which is compounded consists of separate parts which come together to make a whole. However, because God was before everything else there can have been no separate parts to come together to make God. Hence God must be simple.

To put the same thing another way, the doctrine of divine simplicity affirms the truth that God is ontologically basic. There wasn't something more basic than God out of which God was created because God is the creator of everything. In the beginning there was just God and so everything that God is must simply be God.

If it is suggested that something was added to God subsequently the same issue of the cause of divine complexity would arise. Where would this additional thing come from? If God caused it to come into existence then it would be part of creation and not God and if it always existed then there would be another form of eternal existence alongside God, which would be contrary to the biblical teaching that everything either is God or was created by him.

The only thing that makes sense is to say that God not only was, but eternally is, simply God.

If everything that God is, is God, it follows that God is identical with all his attributes. It is not that God is uncreated and also incomprehensible and also eternal. Rather God is one single simple essence that we describe under the separate attributes of being uncreated, incomprehensible and eternal (just as we also say he is holy, wise and loving) because that is the

---

[88] Stephen Charnock, *The Existence and Attributes of God*, 1.333, quoted in Peter Sanlon, *Simply God* (Nottingham: IVP, 2014), Kindle edition Loc 685.

language that has been given to us to make sense of his one single, simple, nature in terms that we can begin to understand.

In similar fashion, if we turn to the divine names, such as God, Lord and Almighty the doctrine of divine simplicity teaches us that God is not God and also Lord and also Almighty. God is just God and the names which we use to describe him (including the name God) are simply different ways that have been given to us to describe his one divine being.

Because God is a single, simple, nature or essence it follows that the Father, the Son and the Holy Spirit must possess this single, simple, nature in its entirety. If they did not do so then they would not be God. Describing them as having the same attributes and possessing the same divine names (as the Athanasian Creed does) is a way of affirming this truth since, as we have said, the divine attributes and the divine names are ways of referring to the one divine nature which the Father, Son and Holy Spirit equally possess.

Because God is simple in the way just described, the affirmation that the Father, Son and the Holy Spirit are God means that each of them possesses the single divine nature in its entirety. That is what it means for them to be God.[89]

The Divine Relations (verses 21–26)

[21]The Father is made of none: neither created, nor begotten. [22]The Son is of the Father alone: not made, nor created, but begotten. [23]The Holy Ghost is of the Father and of the Son: neither made, nor created, nor begotten, but proceeding. [24]So there is one Father, not three Fathers; one Son, not three Sons: one Holy Ghost, not three Holy Ghosts. [25]And in this Trinity none is afore, or after other: none is greater, or less than another; [26]But the whole three Persons are co-eternal together: and co-equal.

The fact that divine simplicity means that the three persons of the Trinity possess one simple divine nature leads to the obvious question. 'How then are the persons of the Trinity distinct from one another?'

---

[89] For helpful introductions to the doctrine of divine simplicity see James Dolezal, *God without Parts* (Eugene: Pickwick, 2011) and Steven Duby, *Divine Simplicity* (London and New York: T&T Clark, 2016).

As Augustine explains in the following passage from his book *The City of God*, in which he refers to God as 'this Good,' the answer to this question is that they are distinct from one another not in terms of their nature, but in terms of their relations to each other:

> This Trinity is one God; the fact that it is a Trinity does not mean that it is not simple. For when we speak of this Good as being by nature simple, we do not mean that it consists solely of the Father, or solely of the Son, or solely of the Holy Spirit, or that there is really only a nominal Trinity, without subsistent Persons; that is the notion of the Sabellian heretics. What is meant by 'simple' is that its being is identical with its attributes apart from the relation in which each person is said to stand with each other. For the Father of course has the Son; and yet he himself is not the Son; and the Son has the Father; and yet he himself is not the Father. But when each is regarded in himself, not in relation to the other, his being is identical with his attributes. Thus each in himself is said to be living, because he *has* life; and at the same time he himself *is* life.[90]

To quote Peter Sanlon, in this passage:

> ... Augustine realizes that the relations of the Trinity are an exception to the key teaching of simplicity. It is not the mere fact of threeness that creates the exception to simplicity; it is the inherent, inescapable other-person-centred relationality of the Father, Son and Spirit.
>
> The Son, considered as the Son, cannot be contained within the core definition of simplicity, because a Son requires a Father. A being is simple if it is its attributes. Simplicity denies dependency and speaks of self-sufficiency. The Threeness of the Trinity involves three persons in mutual relational dependence. The Father would not be the Father without the Son. The Son would not be the Son without the Father. The Spirit would not

---

[90] Augustine, *The City of God*, XI:10 (Harmondsworth: Penguin, 1981), 440–441.

be the Spirit of the Father and the Son without the Father and the Son. The exceptions to simplicity are the relationships that form the mutual intimacy between Father, Son and Spirit.[91]

Verses 21–26 of the Athanasian Creed follow Augustine in seeing the distinction between the persons of the Trinity as consisting in the relations between them. The reason why there is, as verse 24 says, one Father not three, one Son and not three and one Holy Spirit and not three, is because the Father alone is the Father because he alone is 'made of none: neither created, nor begotten,' the Son alone is the Son because he alone is 'of the Father alone: not made, nor created, but begotten' and the Holy Spirit alone is the Holy Spirit because he alone 'is of the Father and of the Son: neither made, nor created, nor begotten, but proceeding' (verses 21–23). As God none of the three persons are made or created, but the persons are distinct because the Father is not begotten, the Son is begotten and Spirit is not begotten but proceeds.

When the Creed follows John 1:14 and Hebrews 1:5 and talks about the Son being 'begotten' by the Father it does not mean that the Father brought the Son into existence through an act of sexual intercourse like those attributed to the gods and goddesses of pagan religion. What it does mean is that the Son derives his being from the Father and therefore possesses the divine nature in the same way that human children possess human nature because they derive their being from their parents.

This point is helpfully explained by the nineteenth-century Anglican theologian Harold Browne. He notes that

> ... our Lord speaks of Himself, as deriving His own eternal Being from God the Father. 'As the living Father hath sent Me, and I live by the Father' (John 6:57), and again, 'As the Father hath life in Himself, so hath He given to the Son to have life in Himself' (John 5:26).[92]

---

[91] Sanlon, *Simply God*, Loc. 908.
[92] E. H. Browne, *An Exposition of the Thirty-Nine Articles* (London: John W Parker, 1854), 65–66.

What we learn from these words, he says, is that:

> ... the mode of existence, which the Father possessed from all eternity, He communicated to the Son. All created beings have their existence from, and their life in God. But the Son, who is uncreated, derives indeed His being from the Father; but it is a Being of the same kind as the Father's, and therefore not dependent, like a creature's, but independent, self-existent, having life in itself.[93]

In line with this, in the New Testament:

> ... the Son is farther called 'the Brightness of His Father's glory, the express Image of His Person,' Heb. 1:3; words, which in the Greek indicate a relation of the Son to His Father, like that of brightness to light, like that of the impression of a seal on wax to the seal, which it answers to.[94]

To be the 'brightness of the Father's glory' and the 'express image of his person' means that the Son has to possess the same self-existent divine nature as the Father and to say he is 'begotten' means that he receives this nature from the Father in the same way that a beam of light receives its origin from a light source.

When the Creed talks about the Spirit as 'proceeding' it does not mean that he moves from one place to another. As the incomprehensible God, the Spirit is in all places at all times (Psalm 139: 7–8) and so cannot proceed in this way. What it means is that as the Son is God because he has his divine nature from the Father, so the Holy Spirit is God because he has his divine nature from the Father and the Son.

This point is helpfully explained by the seventeenth-century theologian John Pearson who declares in his commentary on the Apostles' Creed that the Holy Spirit 'is the most high and eternal God, of the same nature, attributes, and operations with the Father and the Son, by proceeding from them both' and that 'this procession of the Spirit in reference to the

---

[93] Browne, *Thirty Nine Articles*, 66.
[94] Browne, *Thirty Nine Articles*, 66.

Father is delivered expressly, in relation to the Son is contained virtually, in the scriptures.'[95]

Concerning the procession of the Spirit from the Father, Pearson notes that in John 15:26 Christ expressly teaches that the Holy Spirit proceeds from the Father: 'But when the Counselor comes, whom I shall send to you from the Father, even the Spirit of truth, who proceeds from the Father, he will bear witness to me.'

Furthermore, he argues, what is taught in this verse makes sense in view of what we know about the nature of the Trinity in general. The Father and the Spirit share the same divine nature. However, they are different because of the relationship of origin that exists between them, and because the Father does not have his origin from the Spirit, 'it followeth that the Spirit hath it from him.'[96]

Concerning the procession from the Son, Pearson concedes that 'it be not expressly spoken in the scripture that the Holy Ghost proceedeth from the Son.' However, he argues, 'the substance of the same truth is virtually contained here.' This is because the same language that is used to describe the Spirit's relation to the Father as a result of the fact that he proceeds from the Father is also used to describe the Spirit's relation to the Son.

Pearson notes that in Matthew 10:20 the Spirit is called 'the Spirit of your Father' and in 1 Corinthians 2:11–12 he is called 'the Spirit of God,' and that in the same way the Spirit is called 'the Spirit of his Son' in Galatians 4:6 and 'the Spirit of Christ,' or 'the Spirit of Jesus Christ' in Romans 8:2, 1 Peter 1:11 and Philippians 1:9.

The significance of this identity of language, declares Pearson, is that:

> If ... the Holy Spirit be called the Spirit of God and the Father, because he proceedeth from the Father, it followeth that, being called also the Spirit of the Son, he proceedeth also from the Son.[97]

---

[95] Pearson, *An Exposition of the Creed*, 490.
[96] Pearson, *An Exposition of the Creed*, 490–491.
[97] Pearson, *An Exposition of the Creed*, 491.

The Theology of the Athanasian Creed

To put it simply, in both cases 'of' means 'proceeds' and therefore the biblical witness tells us that the Spirit proceeds also from the Son.

This biblical evidence referred to by Pearson means that we need to resist the current ecumenical pressure to return to the original form of the Nicene Creed and say that the Spirit proceeds from the Father alone.

We can agree with the Eastern Christian tradition that according to Scripture the Father is the fount of deity, the one from whom both the Son and the Spirit have their eternally self-existent being. Therefore we have to say that the Holy Spirit is the Spirit of the Father who proceeds from the Father.

However, we also have to say with the Western tradition reflected in the Athanasian Creed that the Spirit does not have his being apart from the Son, but has his being from both the Father and the Son. He is the Spirit of the Son as well as the Spirit of the Father. Therefore we have to say that the Spirit proceeds from the Son as well as from the Father. In the words of Augustine 'as the Father has in Himself that the Holy Spirit should proceed from Him, so has He given to the Son that the same Holy Spirit should proceed from Him.'[98]

It is because the Holy Spirit proceeds from the Father and the Son that he is God and it is because he proceeds rather than is begotten that he is the Spirit rather than a second Son. The Athanasian Creed does not explain the difference between begetting and proceeding and in this it follows the wider Christian tradition which has confessed that the precise difference between the two is difficult to determine. As John of Damascus famously put it in the eighth century, 'we have learned that there is a

---

[98] Augustine, *On The Trinity*, XV.48 in the Nicene and Post Nicene Fathers, 1st series Vol. III (Edinburgh and Grand Rapids, T&T Clark/Eerdmans 1998) p.225. For a more detailed discussion of the debate about the procession of the Holy Spirit see Tom Smail, *The Giving Gift* (London: Hodder & Stoughton, 1988), Ch.5 and The World Council of Churches, *Spirit of God, Spirit of Christ* (Geneva and London: WCC/SPCK, 1981). As Smail notes, the Western emphasis on the relationship between the Spirit and the Son is 'part of the gospel as given and is needed as bulwark against the Christless mysticism, religious pluralism and charismatic excess which can easily intrude when we try to enter into life in the Spirit as something apart from life in the Son' (Smail, *The Giving Gift*, p.132).

difference between generation and procession, but the nature of that difference we in no way understand.'[99]

However, theologians have nevertheless tried to make some sense of this distinction. One of the ways that they have done this is to build on the biblical idea of the Spirit as the breath of God (Genesis 2:7, Psalm 33:6, Ezekiel 37:1–14, John 20:22) by talking about the procession of the Spirit as meaning that the Spirit is breathed out by the Father in distinction to the Son being begotten by Him.

As Tom Smail explains in his book *The Giving Gift*, this way of understanding what is meant by the procession of the Holy Spirit is a helpful way to begin to make sense of what is distinctive about the Spirit over against the Son.

In his view, the begetting of the Son:

> ... is like a human begetting, in that it results in the production of another centre of personal life who is of the same 'stuff' as his Father, but who stands over against him as a second person distinct from him. They are one in their deity; yet, like any parent and child they are sufficiently distinct for the one to love and be loved by the other.[100]

On the other hand, the procession of the Spirit:

> ... is more like the production of a divine breath that carries within it God's being, life, truth and power. In the Son the Father finds a partner for his love and in the Spirit he finds a way of communicating that love first to the Son and then to us. The Son is the primary object of the Father's love: it makes good New Testament sense to say 'The Father loves the Son' (John 5:20). However, there is no equivalent statement that 'The Father loves the Spirit,' for that would be an inappropriate thing to say. The Spirit

---

[99] John of Damascus, *Exposition of the Orthodox Faith*, Ch VIII in *The Nicene and Post Nicene Fathers*, 2nd series, vol. IX (Grand Rapids: Eerdmans, 1997), 9.
[100] Smail, *The Giving Gift*, 122.

is not the personal *object* of the Father's love, but rather its personal *communication*. The special relationship of the Spirit to the Father's love is expressed in Romans 5:5: 'God has poured out his love into our hearts by the Holy Spirit whom he has given us.'[101]

In summary, says Smail:

> The difference between the begetting of the Son and the breathing out of the Spirit has something to do with the difference between originating someone to love and originating someone else by whom that love can be conveyed.[102]

In these quotations Smail focuses on the way in which the Spirit communicates the Father's love to the Son and though him to us. However, this is only half the picture. According to the New Testament, the Son, and through him we ourselves, also love the Father in return ('We love because he first loved us' 1 John 4:19) and it is the Spirit who also communicates this responsive love. In the words of the title of a book by the late John Taylor, the Spirit is the 'go-between God'[103] who is the personal expression of *both* the Father's paternal love for the Son *and* the Son's filial love for the Father. Because we are 'in the Son' this also means that the Spirit is the personal expression of the Father's love to us and of our responsive love to the Father (see Romans 5:5, 8:14-15 and Galatians 4:5-6).

It is because the persons are distinguished by their relations in the way just described, says the Creed, 'there is one Father, not three Fathers; one Son, not three Sons: one Holy Ghost, not three Holy Ghosts.' What makes each person distinct means also that there is only one of them.

- There is only one Father because only the Father is neither begotten nor proceeds, but begets the Son and causes the Spirit to proceed.
- There is only one Son because only the Son is begotten by the Father and causes the Spirit to proceed.

---

[101] Smail, *The Giving Gift*, 122.
[102] Smail, *The Giving Gift*, 122.
[103] John V. Taylor, *The Go-Between God* (London: SCM, 1975).

- There is only one Spirit because only the Spirit proceeds from the Father and the Son.

Just in case its explanation of the distinction between the persons might seem to give room to the Arian idea that the Son and the Spirit somehow possess a lesser former of deity than that possessed by the Father, the Creed then re-iterates in verses 25–26 that 'in this Trinity none is afore, or after other: none is greater, or less than another; But the whole three Persons are co-eternal together: and co-equal.'

As Waterland explains, we should not understand the phrase 'none is afore or after another' in terms of the order which exists within the Trinity by reason of the relations between the Persons because with regard to these 'the Father is first, the Son second, and Holy Ghost third in order.' Nor should we understand it in terms of the offices, or roles, which the Persons perform 'for the Father is supreme in office, while the Son and the Spirit condescend to inferior offices.'[104] Instead we are

> ... to understand it, as the Creed itself explains it, of duration and of dignity; in which respect none is afore or after, none greater or less, but the whole three Persons, coeternal and coequal.[105]

By stressing that 'none is afore or after,' but that all three persons of the Trinity are coeternal the Creed detaches the issue of causation from time. In this world a cause must always exist before an effect. In the same way, argued the Arians the Father must have existed before Son and therefore there must have been a time when the Son did not exist. Hence the famous Arian slogan concerning the Son 'there was when he was not.' The orthodox response to this argument, which the Athanasian Creed reflects, is that as God exists outside time in him causation and time are not linked. The Father is the cause of the existence of the Son and the Spirit and the Son is the cause of the existence of the Spirit, but this causation is something eternal. To use two images employed by the Fathers, it is like water eternally pouring forth from a spring or light eternally steaming forth from a lamp.

---

[104] Waterland, *A Critical History*, 144. For a detailed discussion of the distinction of order and office in the Trinity see Michael Ovey, *Your Will Be Done* (London: Latimer Trust, 2016).
[105] Waterland, *A Critical History*, 144.

Conclusion of the Account of the Trinity (verses 27–28)

²⁷So that in all things, as is aforesaid: the Unity in Trinity, and the Trinity in Unity is to be worshipped. ²⁸He therefore that will be saved: must thus think of the Trinity.

Returning to the point where his discussion of the Trinity began, the author of the Creed concludes this section in verses 27–28 by declaring once again that the Catholic faith is that 'the Unity in Trinity, and the Trinity in Unity is to be worshipped.' Because this is the Catholic faith, and because, for the reasons discussed above, salvation involves holding fast to the Catholic faith, it follows that 'He therefore that will be saved: must thus think of the Trinity.'

The Significance of What We Learn About the Trinity in Verses 3–28

A common reaction that people have when introduced to the sort of teaching about the Trinity that is found in verses 3–28 of the Athanasian Creed is to say 'Yes, but why does it matter?'

The answer to this question is that these verses teach us three key things that enable us to understand rightly who the God of the Bible is.

First, they teach us that God is both absolute and personal. God is absolute in the sense that as the one eternal and uncreated God who is Father, Son and Holy Spirit he is 'self-existent, self-sufficient and self-contained, not relying on anything outside himself for his existence.'[106] Furthermore, as the use of the word 'his' indicates, God is not an impersonal force, but as Father, Son and Holy Spirit personal in himself and as such the origin of personhood in other personal creatures such as angels and human beings. Why do we and everything else exist? Because of the existence of the absolute creator God. Why do we exist as personal beings? Because this absolute creator God is personal as Father, Son and Holy Spirit.

---

[106] Christopher Watkin, *Thinking Through Creation* (Phillipsburg: P&R, 2017), 24.

As the American apologist John Frame argues, it is the fact that biblical God is both absolute and personal that distinguishes him from the deities described by non-biblical religions:

> The major religions of the world, in their most typical, (one tends to say 'authentic') forms, are either pantheistic (Hinduism, Taoism) or polytheistic (animism, some forms of Hinduism, Shinto, and the traditional religions of Greece, Rome, Egypt, etc.). Pantheism has an absolute, but not a personal absolute. Polytheism has personal gods, but none of these is absolute. Indeed, although most religions tend to emphasize either pantheistic absolutism or personal non-absolutism, we can usually find both elements beneath the surface. In Greek polytheism, for example, the gods are personal but non-absolute. Yet this polytheism is supplemented by a doctrine of fate, which is a kind of impersonal absolute. Similarly, behind the gods of animism is Mana, the impersonal reality. People seem to have a desire for both personality and absoluteness, but in most religions these two elements are separated and therefore compromise each other, rather than reinforcing each other. Thus, of the major religious movements, only biblical religion calls us with clarity to worship a personal absolute.[107]

Secondly, an important aspect of the absolute nature of God is that as Father, Son and Holy Spirit God is eternally relational in himself and therefore does not need anything outside himself to fulfil his personal, relational character. In the words of Christopher Watkin:

> God is not first of all a single person who then enters into relationship with other persons, his being is relational from the very beginning. One important consequence of this primordial relationality is that God did not need to create the universe in general, or human beings in particular, in order to have something or someone to keep him company. God was enjoying perfectly loving, mutually glorifying relationships before any act of

---

[107] John M. Frame, *Apologetics: A Justification of Christian Belief* (Phillipsburg: P&R, 2015), 37.

creation took place. God chose to create the universe, but he did not need to do so in order to be who he is. He does not need us.[108]

To use a distinction made by C S Lewis in his book *The Four Loves*, this means that God's actions in creation and redemption are thus not motivated by 'need love.' God does not create and save us because he needs, in order to fulfil his own self, to either love us, or for us to love him. God's actions are instead forms of 'gift love.' They are acts motivated by a desire to benefit another. In Lewis' words 'In God there is no hunger that needs to be filled, only plenteousness that desires to give.'[109]

Thirdly, in the words of Karl Barth, as the God who is eternally Father, Son and Holy Spirit, 'God is, so to speak, ours in advance.'[110] God can create us as Father, Son and Holy Spirit because he is Father, Son and Holy Spirit, and likewise it is because he is Father, Son and Holy Spirit that he can save us from our rebellion against him. As the Church of England Doctrine Commission report *The Mystery of Salvation* puts it, the doctrine of the Trinity tells us:

> ... that God is his own divine self really is such that God can share himself with his creation. God is not only the utterly other who infinitely transcends creation; God can also be deeply and intimately present within creation, as the Spirit, and God can also be one of us, a genuinely human person, as Jesus Christ the Son. Therefore God can and does open up his own life for us to share. Moreover, because God is Trinity God can share his life even with those created beings, ourselves, who are alienated from God and opposed to God. As incarnate Son and indwelling Spirit, God enters our situation of evil, suffering and mortality, shares with us the pain of our alienation, bears for us the pain of overcoming our enmity and healing our estrangement, sustains us in the struggle to be truly human, redirects our lives towards the Father

---

[108] Watkin, *Thinking Through Creation*, 32.
[109] C. S. Lewis, *The Four Loves* (Glasgow: Fontana, 1965), 116.
[110] Karl Barth, *Church Dogmatics* I/1 (London and New York: T&T Clark, 2004), 383.

as the source and goal of our being. The New Testament summary narratives of Trinitarian self-giving imply all this. It is as Father, Son and Holy Spirit that God can and does save us.[III]

Introduction to the Account of the Incarnation (verses 29–30)

²⁹Furthermore it is necessary to everlasting salvation: that he also believe rightly the Incarnation of our Lord Jesus Christ. ³⁰For the right Faith is that we believe and confess: that our Lord Jesus Christ, the Son of God, is God and Man.

The teaching of the Catholic faith is not only that 'the Word was with God, and was God' (John 1:18), but that 'the Word became flesh and dwelt among us' (John 1:14). Consequently the Creed follows its account of the Catholic faith with regard to the Trinity with an account of the Catholic faith with regard to the incarnation. Verses 29 and 30 introduce this account in the same way that verses 1-4 introduced the teaching on the Trinity.

Verse 29 begins this introduction by making the point that it is not enough to hold to the Catholic faith with regard to the Trinity without also upholding the Catholic faith concerning the incarnation. If anyone wants to be saved it is also necessary that they 'believe rightly the Incarnation of our Lord Jesus Christ.' 'Rightly' here means 'in accordance with the Catholic faith.' Verse 30 then specifies that what this means is that they must believe (and therefore confess) 'that our Lord Jesus Christ, the Son of God is God and Man.' The fact that the Word became flesh as a male human being means that the word 'Man' does a double duty, signifying that Jesus Christ was and is 'Man' in the sense of human and 'man' in the sense of a man rather than a woman.

God and Man (verses 31–33)

³¹God, of the Substance of the Father, begotten before the worlds: and Man, of the Substance of his Mother, born in the world; ³²Perfect God, and Perfect Man: of a reasonable soul and human flesh subsisting;

[III]The Doctrine Commission of the Church of England, *The Mystery of Salvation* (London: CHP, 1995), 43.

³³Equal to the Father, as touching his Godhead: and inferior to the Father, as touching his Manhood.

These verses explain what it means to say that Jesus Christ is God and Man. First of all, verse 31 follows what was said about God the Son in the Trinitarian section of the Creed by declaring that the Son who became incarnate is 'God, of the Substance of the Father, begotten before the worlds.' Why is he God? Because he is begotten from the Father. When did this generation take place? Eternally, hence 'before the worlds.'

Verse 31 then goes on to say that just as Jesus Christ is God by reason of his eternal generation from the Father, so also he is human by reason of having received his humanity from the humanity of the Virgin Mary through the miraculous action of the Holy Spirit. As Luke tells us:

> And the angel said to her, 'Don't be afraid Mary, for you have found favour with God. And behold you will conceive in your womb and bear a son, and you shall call his name Jesus …. The Holy Spirit shall come upon you, and the power of the Most High will overshadow you; therefore the child to be born will be called holy, the Son of God' (Luke 1:30–31).

As we saw when looking at the teaching of the Creed on the Trinity, the Son who became incarnate is, as verse 32 says 'perfect God.' The simplicity of God means that being God by reason of his generation from the Father, the Son possesses all that God is. Once again this rules out the Arian belief that the Son was some inferior form of deity.

Not only is the Son eternally perfect God, but by reason of the incarnation he also, verse 32 says, 'became perfect Man.' In the words of Hebrews 2:17, the Son was 'made like his brethren in every respect.' The second half of verse 32 glosses what 'perfect Man' means by saying that it means that the incarnate Son is 'of a reasonable soul and human flesh subsisting.' This gloss rules out as incompatible with Catholic faith the fourth century heresy known as Apollinarianism which held that the divine Word took the place of Christ's human soul.[112] Human beings are a compound of body and soul, so if Christ did not have a human soul it

---

[112] For details about Apollinarianism see J. N. D. Kelly *Early Christian Doctrines*, 5ed (London: A&C Black, 1980), 289–295.

follows that the Son would not have been 'made like his brethren in every respect.'

Verse 33 then goes on to explain that the Catholic faith that the incarnate Christ is both God and Man means that he is both equal and inferior to the Father. Over against the Arians the verse insists once again that he is equal to the Father in respect of the common divine nature possessed by the Father and the Son. However, just as all human beings, as creatures, are inferior to the God who created them, so also the human nature of Christ is inferior to the deity of the Father. Augustine helpfully expounds this point in his handbook on Christian doctrine, *The Enchiridion on Faith, Hope and Love* with reference to St Paul's teaching in Philippians 2:7 about Christ taking on the 'form of a servant':

> But he made Himself of no reputation and took upon Himself the form of a servant, not losing or lessening the form of God. And, accordingly, He was both made less and remained equal, being both in one, as has been said: but He was one of these as Word, and the other as man. As Word, He is equal with the Father; as man, less than the Father.[113]

How the Relation of Christ's Divinity and Humanity is to Be Understood (verses 34–37)

34 Who although he be God and Man: yet he is not two, but one Christ; 35 One, not by conversion of the Godhead into flesh: but by taking of the Manhood into God; 36 One altogether, not by confusion of Substance: but by unity of Person. 37 For as the reasonable soul and flesh is one man: so God and Man is one Christ.

Having declared in verses 30–33 that Jesus Christ is both God and Man, the Creed continues by explaining how he is nevertheless the one person who was born, died, rose, ascended, is seated at God's right hand and will come again in glory to judge the living and the dead.

Verse 34 introduces the section by stating the key truth that all though Christ 'be God and Man: yet he is not two, but one Christ.' If we ask why it needed to be said that Christ is not two but one, the answer is that at

---

[113] Augustine, *Enchiridion* 35, in *The Nicene and Post Nicene Fathers*, First Series, Vol. III (Edinburgh and Grand Rapids: T&T Clark/Eerdmans), 249.

this point the Creed is rebutting a heresy known as Nestorianism. In response to the idea that the Virgin Mary should be regarded as the *theotokos* (the Mother of God) by reason of the union of God and Man in Christ, this heresy held that Christ should be seen in terms of a union of a human being and the second person of the Trinity 'by harmony of will and by divine favour.'[114]

Understanding that this section has Nestorianism in view makes sense of the rejection in verses 35 and 36 of the 'conversion of the Godhead into flesh' and 'confusion of substance.' As Kelly explains, the Nestorians contended that their opponents 'extreme insistence on the unity of the God-man' had to involve either 'a change in the Divine Word' such that the Word became human rather than divine, or a confusion between the divine and human natures.[115] This criticism was potentially damaging because the ideas that God became Man by somehow ceasing to be God, or that the divine and human natures somehow became confused together, both undercut the teaching of the Catholic faith that Christ was both truly divine and truly human ('Perfect God and Perfect Man'). The first would mean that he ceased to be truly God and the second that he was neither truly God nor truly Man, but had some third kind of nature which was a combination of aspects of both (a scenario which would make Christ more than human but less than God).

As Kelly goes on to say, the orthodox response to this Nestorian criticism was to say that 'the unity for which they contended was to be found in the Lord's person.'[116] In line with this response, verse 36 of the Athanasian Creed says that Christ is one 'by unity of person.'

When the Creed goes on to say in verse 37 'For as the reasonable soul and flesh is one man: so God and Man is one Christ' the use of the word 'for' indicates that this analogy explains what 'unity of person' means. In the *Enchiridion* Augustine writes 'just as each individual man unites in one person a body and rational soul, so Christ in one person unites the Word and man'[117] and the Creed is making the same point. In a human being, it says, there is a single person who possesses both a material body and

---

[114] Kelly, *Early Christian Doctrines*, 17. For further details on Nestorianism see 310–317.
[115] Kelly, *The Athanasian Creed*, 96-97.
[116] Kelly, *The Athanasian Creed*, 97.
[117] Augustine, *Enchiridion* 36, 250.

an immaterial soul and in Christ there is one person who possesses both God's nature and Man's nature.

The Council of Chalcedon in 451 produced a statement of faith about Christology which has become the standard of mainstream Christian orthodoxy on the matter. This statement, The Chalcedonian Confession, runs as follows:

> Following the holy Fathers we teach with one voice that the Son [of God] and our Lord Jesus Christ is to be confessed as one and the same [Person], that he is perfect in Godhead and perfect in manhood, very God and very man, of a reasonable soul and [human] body consisting, consubstantial with the Father, as touching his Godhead, and consubstantial with us as touching his manhood; made in all things like unto us, sin only excepted; begotten of his Father before the worlds according to his godhead; but in these last days for us men and for our salvation born [into the world] of the Virgin Mary, the mother of God according to his manhood. This one and the same Jesus Christ, the only-begotten Son [of God] must be confessed to be in two natures, unconfusedly, immutably, indivisibly, inseparably [united], and that without the distinction of natures being taken away by such union, but rather the peculiar property of each nature being preserved and being united in one Person and one subsistence, not separated or divided into two persons, but one and the same Son and only-begotten, God the Word, our Lord Jesus Christ, as the Prophets of old time have spoken concerning him, and as the Lord Jesus Christ hath taught us, and as the Creed of the Fathers hath delivered to us.[118]

---

[118] Text in *Nicene and Post Nicene Fathers,* vol. XIV (Edinburgh & Grand Rapids: T&T Clark/Eerdmans, 1997), 264–265.

Although the Athanasian Creed does not use the precise terminology contained in the *Confession*, it is making the same theological point. In Christ there are two natures united by being the natures of one person.

When in verse 35 the Creed talks about 'the taking of Manhood into God' the truth this phrase expresses is that the person who united the two natures with himself was God the Son, the second Person of the Trinity who, possessing the divine nature from all eternity, assumed human nature at the incarnation, thereby taking humanity into the life of God.

As Article II of the *Thirty-Nine Articles* puts it:

> The Son, which is the Word of the Father, begotten from everlasting of the Father, the very and eternal God, and of one substance with the Father, took man's nature in the womb of the blessed Virgin, of her substance: so that two whole and perfect natures, that is to say, the Godhead and manhood, were joined together in one person, never to be divided, whereof is one Christ, very God and very man, who truly suffered, was crucified, dead, and buried, to reconcile His Father to us, and to be a sacrifice, not only for original guilt, but also for all actual sins of men.

That it is the eternal Son of God who is the person who unites the two natures of Christ is made clear by the New Testament. Throughout the New Testament there is one person described or referred to, never two, and if we ask who that person was, the answer is, as we have already indicated, that it was the eternal Word or Son of God who took human nature upon Himself at the incarnation (John 1:14). It was the one who was rich with the glory of heaven who became poor for our sake (2 Corinthians 8:9). It was the one who 'descended' from heaven to earth at the incarnation who ascended 'far above all the heavens' (Ephesians 4:9–10). It was the one who was eternally 'in the form of God' who 'emptied himself', took upon himself 'the form of a servant' and was 'born in the likeness of men' (Phil 2:7). It was the one who 'reflects the glory of God and bears the very stamp of his nature, upholding the universe by his word of power' who partook of our nature for the sake of our salvation (Hebrews 1:3 and 2:14–18).

At this point someone might object that God is always simply God. How then can humanity be added to who God is?' This is a reasonable question and there is a reasonable answer to it. The answer is that God exists outside of time. For us the incarnation is an event in time with a before and after. Prior to the action of the Holy Spirit leading Mary to conceive the Word was not incarnate. After that action he was. For God, however, being outside of time, the incarnation is an eternal part of who he is. The second Person of the Trinity is eternally God incarnate. That is why St. Paul can talk in Ephesians 1:4 about Christians being chosen in Christ 'before the foundation of the world' and why St. John likewise refers in Revelation 13:8 to 'the Lamb slain before the foundation of the world.'

To use technical theological terminology, the fact that the eternal Son is the Person who unites the two natures of Christ means that Christ's human nature is *anhypostatic* – that is to say, the human nature is without (Greek *an)* a human person (Greek *hypostasis*). There was (and is) no human 'I' separate from the eternal Son who could say 'this is my nature.' As Oliver Crisp puts it: 'the human nature of Christ does not at any time compose an existing individual human person apart from the Word.'[119]

Instead, Christ's human nature was *enhypostatic. En* in Greek means 'in' and so saying that Christ's human nature was *enhypostatic* means that *it exists in* the person of the eternal second person of the Trinity. In the words of Fred Sanders:

> ... the human nature of Jesus Christ is in fact a nature joined to a person, and therefore enhypostatic, or personalized. But the person who personalizes the human nature of Christ is not a created human person (like all the other persons personalizing the other human natures we encounter); rather it is the eternal second person of the Trinity. So the human nature of Christ is personal, but with a personhood from above.[120]

---

[119] Oliver Crisp, *Divinity and Humanity* (Cambridge: CUP, 2007), 87.
[120] Quoted by David Mathis in 'Enhypostasis: What kind of flesh did the Word become?' at https://www.desiringgod.org/articles/enhypostasis-what-kind-of-flesh-did-the-word-become (Accessed 8 April 2019).

It is sometimes objected that if the human nature possessed by Christ was not attached to a human person then Christ was not truly human. For example, Anthony and Richard Hanson write:

> What we encounter in Jesus Christ, according to the orthodox view, is not *a* man, but a non-personal humanity, a humanity that is expressed, not in a human person, but in the divine mode of being, God the Word. It is moreover true that orthodox doctrine has nearly always taught that what God the Word assumed at the incarnation was not personal humanity, but impersonal humanity. Strictly speaking, orthodox doctrine is not that God became *a* man, but that God became man. The critics would object that impersonal humanity is a contradiction in terms. The essence of humanity is to be personal. If God in Jesus Christ assumed impersonal humanity, the incarnation was not a manifestation of God in real humanity.[121]

The answer to this objection is that the critics have not understood orthodox teaching properly. It has never been taught that in Christ there was an impersonal humanity, a human nature unattached to a person. Rather it has been held that from the moment of conception the humanity of Christ *was* personal in that it was the humanity of the second Person of the Trinity.

Moreover, As H M Relton argues, the fact that the person involved was God the Son does not make Christ's humanity any less human. God is not less personal than we are, but more so, and as those made in God's image our personhood is a reflection of the divine archetype. It follows, says Relton, that the incarnation of the Son:

> ... brought to the human nature he assumed, not an alien element such as would render a truly human life for the God-man an impossibility, but just that which alone could make the life of Christ in every stage of its growth and development a truly and perfectly human life. The Divine

---

[121] Anthony Hanson and Richard Hanson, *Reasonable Faith* (Oxford: OUP, 1981), 90. Italics original.

> Logos was capable of being the Ego, not only of His Divine but also of His Human Nature; because His Personality in virtue of its Divinity already embraced all that is most distinctive of a truly human personality. The human and the Divine are not two contradictory, but two complementary terms, and the less is contained in the greater. His Divine self-consciousness was, in virtue of its Divinity, a truly human self-consciousness. His ego was Divine – it was also human; therefore it could be the subject of both natures.[122]

In summary, what verses 29–37 of the Athanasian Creed teach us is that to adhere to the Catholic faith we must believe that God came to dwell among us in one the person of the God-Man Jesus Christ. In the words of Barth, we must believe:

> This Jesus of Nazareth, who passes through the cities and villages of Galilee and wanders to Jerusalem, who is there accused and condemned and crucified, this man is the Jehovah of the Old Testament, is the Creator, is God Himself. A man like us in space and time, who has all the properties of God and yet does not cease to be a human being and a creature too. The Creator Himself, without encroaching upon His deity, becomes, not a demi-god, not an angel, but very soberly, very really a man.[123]

The Actions of the God-Man

³⁸ Who suffered for our salvation: descended into hell, rose again the third day from the dead. ³⁹He ascended into heaven, he sitteth on the right hand of the Father, God Almighty: from whence he shall come to judge the quick and the dead.

In line with the witness of the New Testament and of the early Creeds, verses 38 and 39 explain that after his incarnation Christ suffered on the Cross (1 Peter 2:21–24), descended to the dead ('hell' like the original Latin *infera*, meaning the place of the dead, what the Old Testament calls *sheol* (Acts 2:31) , rose again on the third day (1 Corinthians 15:4),

---

[122] H. M. Relton, *A Study in Christology* (London: SPCK, 1934), 227.
[123] Karl Barth, *Dogmatics in Outline* (London: SSM, 1985), 84.

ascended to heaven (Acts 1:9–11), is seated at the right hand of God the Father (Colossians 3:1) and will come from there to judge the living ('the quick') and the dead (Matthew 16:27).

The word 'Who' at the beginning of verse 38 links what is said in these two verses with the account of the person of Christ given in verses 30–37. It is the 'one Christ' who is both God and Man who did, and will do, everything that is listed in verses 38–39. It is God the Son, the second person of the Trinity, who suffered, died, rose, ascended and will come again in judgement. However, all these actions by God the Son involve the human nature which he assumed at the incarnation. He suffered and died in his human nature, the resurrection was the bringing back to new life of his human nature, the ascension was the ascension into heaven of his human nature, and according to Acts 1:11 his coming again will involve his return in his human nature.

The Necessity for the Incarnation

The teaching of verses 29–39 of the Athanasian Creed raises the issue of the necessity for the incarnation. Why did our salvation involve 'God crossing the frontier to man,' to use Barth's phrase?[124]

A helpful answer to this question is given by Martin Luther in his commentary on the Epistle to the Galatians. Commenting on Galatians 3:13 (Christ redeemed us from the curse of the law, having become a curse for us—for it is written, 'Cursed be everyone who hangs on a tree'") Luther explains first of all that in order for us to be saved our saviour had to be God himself:

> And here ye see how necessary a thing it is to believe and confess the article of the divinity of Christ: which when Arius denied, he must needs also deny the article of our redemption. For to overcome the sin of the world, death, the curse, and the wrath of God in himself, is not the work of any creature, but of the divine power. Therefore he which in himself should overcome these, must needs be truly and naturally God. For against this mighty power of sin, death and the curse (which of itself reigneth

---

[124] Karl Barth, *Church Dogmatics IV.1* (London and New York: T&T Clark, 2004), 82.

> throughout the world and in the whole creature), it was necessary to set a more high and mighty power. But besides the [sovereign and] divine power, no such power can be found. Wherefore, to abolish sin, to destroy death, to take away the curse in himself, and to give righteousness, to bring life to light, and to give the blessing (that is, to reduce these things to nothing and to create these), are the works of the divine power only and alone.[125]

However, as Luther goes on to explain, God's power only became effective for our salvation because in Jesus he took our human nature upon him, identified himself with our sinfulness, and therefore endured the curse which we deserve.

He writes:

> Let us therefore receive this most sweet doctrine and full of comfort, with thanksgiving and with an assured faith, which teacheth that Christ being made a curse for us (that is, a sinner subject to the wrath of God), did put upon him our person, and laid our sins upon his own shoulders, saying: I have committed the sins which all men have committed. Therefore he was made a curse indeed according to the law, not for himself, but (as Paul saith) for us. For unless he had taken upon himself my sins and thine, and the sins of the whole world, the law had no right over him, which condemneth none but sinners only, and holdeth them under the curse. Wherefore he could neither have been made a curse or die, since the only cause of the curse and death is sin, from the which he was free. But because he had taken upon himself our sins, not by constraint, but of his own good will, it behoved him to bear the punishment and wrath of God: not for his own person (which was just and invincible, and therefore could be found in no wise guilty), but for our person.

---

[125] Martin Luther, *A Commentary on St. Paul's Epistle to the Galatians* (Cambridge: James Clarke, 1978), 274.

> So making a happy exchange with us, he took upon him our sinful person, and gave unto us his innocent and victorious person: wherewith we being now clothed, are freed from the curse of the law. For Christ was willingly made a curse for us, saying: As touching my own person, both as human and divine, I am blessed and need nothing; but I will empty myself and will put upon me your person, that is to say, your human nature, and I will walk in the same among you, and will suffer death to deliver you from death. Now he thus bearing the sin of the whole world in our person, was taken, suffered, was crucified and put to death, and became a curse for us. But because he was a person divine and everlasting, it was impossible that death should hold him. Wherefore there is neither sin nor death in him any more, but mere righteousness, life and everlasting blessedness.[126]

In his *Dogmatics in Outline* Barth reiterates the point made by Luther. He declares:

> God Himself, in Jesus Christ His Son, at once true God and true man, takes the place of condemned man. God's judgement is executed, God's law takes its course, but in such a way that what man had to suffer is suffered by this One, who as God's Son stands for all others. Such is the lordship of Jesus Christ, who stands for us before God, by taking upon himself what belongs to us. In Him God makes himself liable, at the point at which we are accursed and guilty and lost. He it is in His Son, who in the person of this crucified man bears on Golgotha all that ought to be laid on us. And in this way he makes an end of the curse.[127]

Why did God cross the frontier into our world? So that by taking our nature upon him and thus identifying himself with us he might bear the curse that our sins deserve. By so doing he broke the power of sin and death and inaugurated for us the new life of righteousness and everlasting

---

[126] Luther, *Galatians*, 275–6.
[127] Barth, *Dogmatics in Outline*, 118–119.

blessedness that is manifested in his resurrection and his ascension to the right hand of God.

When Article XI of the *Thirty-Nine Articles* declares 'We are accounted righteous before God only for the merit of our Lord and Saviour Jesus Christ, and not for our own works of deservings' it points us back to the truth we have just outlined. Why does God account us righteous and therefore eternally blessed? Because in Jesus God crossed the frontier into our world, took our sinfulness upon him, and gave us his righteousness instead. When we respond to the gospel in faith we accept what God has done for us and it thereby becomes ours. In the words of St. Paul 'since all have sinned and fall short of the glory of God, they are justified by his grace as a gift, through the redemption which in Christ Jesus, whom God put forward as an expiation by his blood to be received by faith' (Romans 3:23–25).

The Final Judgement

⁴⁰At whose coming all men shall rise again with their bodies: and shall give account for their own works. ⁴¹And they that have done good shall go into life everlasting: and they that have done evil into everlasting fire.

Theses verses complete the Creed's account of the activity of the God-Man Jesus Christ by describing what will happen when he comes again in judgement.

When verse 40 states that at Christ's coming 'all men shall rise again with their bodies: and shall give account for their own works' it is pointing us to the teaching of Romans 14:12, 1 Corinthians 3:11–15, 2 Corinthians 5:10 and Revelation 20:11–13.

In the first St. Paul states 'So each of us shall give an account of ourselves to God.' In the second he warns that the last judgement will 'test what sort of work each has done.' In the third he declares: 'we must all appear before the judgement seat of Christ, so that each one may receive good or evil, according to what he has done in the body.' Finally, in the fourth St. John tells us:

> Then I saw a great white throne and him who sat upon it; from his presence earth and sky fled away, and no place was found for them. And I saw the dead, great and small,

standing before the throne, and books were opened. Also another book was opened, which is the book of life. And the dead were judged by what was written in the books, by what they had done. And the sea gave up the dead in it, Death and Hades gave up the dead in them, and all were judged by what they had done.

It is important to note that the truth that we shall have to give an account of our works does not call into question the doctrine of justification by faith. In the words of Philip Hughes, commenting on 2 Corinthians 5:10. 'The justification of the sinner, it is true, is by faith in Christ and not by works of his own; but the hidden root of faith must bring forth the visible fruit of good works.'[128] The judgement of what we have done will therefore be the judgement of our faith. Our faith, or lack of it, will be shown by what we did, or failed to do. To quote J I Packer:

> Final judgement, as we saw, will be according to our works – that is, our doings, our whole course of life. The relevance of our 'doings' is not that they ever merit an award from the court – they are too far short of perfection for that – but that they provide an index of what is in the heart – what, in other words, is the real nature of each agent. Jesus once said, 'on the day of judgement men will render account for every careless word they utter; for by your words you will be justified, and by your words you will be condemned' (Matt 12:36f RSV). What is the significance of the words we utter (which utterance is, of course, a 'work' in the relevant sense)? Just this: the words show what you are inside. Jesus had just made this very point. 'The tree is known by its fruit ... how can you speak good, when you are evil? For out of the abundance of the heart the mouth speaks' (verse 33ff.). Similarly, in the sheep-and-goats passage appeal is made to whether men had or had not relieved Christians' needs. What is the significance of that? It is not that one way of acting was meritorious while the other was not, but that from these actions one can tell whether there was love for Christ, the

---

[128] Philip Hughes, *The Second Epistle to the Corinthians* (Grand Rapids: Eerdmans, 1962), 183.

> love that springs from faith, in the heart (see Matt 25:34ff).¹²⁹

The declaration in verse 41 that 'they that have done good shall go into life everlasting: and they that have done evil into everlasting fire' is based on the contrast drawn by Christ himself between the fate of the righteous and the unrighteous in Mathew 25:46.

'Life everlasting' refers to the life of unending joy which the righteous will enjoy with God for ever in the New Jerusalem, the renewed creation (Revelation 21–22). 'Eternal fire' by contrast, is one of series of images used by Christ to indicate the life of unending torment endured by the unrighteous as a consequence of their choice to reject God.

To quote Packer again:

> ... what does it mean to lose our souls? To answer this question, Jesus uses His own solemn imagery – 'Gehenna' (hell in Mark 9:47 and then other gospel texts), the valley outside Jerusalem where rubbish was burned; the 'worm' that 'dieth not' (Mark 9:48), an image, it seems for the endless dissolution of the personality by a condemning conscience; 'fire' for the agonising awareness of God's displeasure; 'outer darkness' for knowledge of the loss, not merely of God, but of all good, and everything that made life seem worth living; 'gnashing of teeth' for self-condemnation and self-loathing. These things are, no doubt, unimaginably dreadful, though those who have been convicted of sin know a little of their nature. But they are not arbitrary inflictions; they represent, rather, a conscious growing into the state in which one has chosen to be. The unbeliever has preferred to be by himself, without God, defying God, having God against him, and he shall have his choice.¹³⁰

---

¹²⁹ J. I. Packer, *Knowing God* (London: Hodder and Stoughton, 1973), 161.
¹³⁰ Packer, *Knowing God*, 169–170.

The Point of the Last Judgement

Many people today have difficulty with the doctrine of the final judgement. They find it difficult to understand why the story of God's saving work reaches its culmination in an act of judgement in the way that the Athanasian Creed describes.

However, the Bible and the Christian tradition view things very differently. They see the final judgement as something good for which we should hope. The reason why this is the case is helpfully explained by the Australian biblical scholar Leon Morris who notes that the doctrine of judgement gives dignity to our actions in this world and the assurance that goodness will in the end triumph over evil.

> The doctrine of final judgment ... stresses man's accountability and the certainty that justice will finally triumph over all the wrongs which are part and parcel of life here and now. The former gives a dignity to the humblest action, the latter brings calmness and assurance to those in the thick of the battle. This doctrine gives meaning to life .... The Christian view of judgement means that history moves to a goal.... Judgment protects the idea of the triumph of God and of good. It is unthinkable that the present conflict between good and evil should last throughout eternity. Judgment means that evil will be disposed of authoritatively, decisively, finally. Judgment means that in the end God's will will be perfectly done.[131]

If we ask how God's will will be perfectly done when people still persist in rejecting him, the answer is that part of God's will is that his human creatures should be persons able to exercise freedom and thus be able to love (enforced love being a contradiction in terms). This freedom involves being able to choose not to love and serve God[132] and, as we have seen, this brings about the possibility of eternal damnation. For this reason,

---

[131] Leon Morris, *The Biblical Doctrine of Judgment* in Packer, *Knowing God*, 159–160.
[132] This is the significance of the gospel accounts of Jesus' temptation. As a free human being he was faced with the choice of whether or not to love and serve his heavenly Father.

eternal damnation, terrible though it is, is a working out of God's good will towards us. It is the consequence of God's good gift of freedom.[133]

A Renewed Warning on the Importance of Adhering to the Catholic Faith

[42]This is the Catholick Faith: which except a man believe faithfully, he cannot be saved.

The Creed ends where it began, with a warning about the paramount importance of adhering to the Catholic faith. Kelly notes that the Latin words '*nisi quis fideliter firmiterque crediderit*' are better translated 'Unless a man believes it faithfully and steadfastly.'[134] This translation brings out more clearly than the Prayer Book translation that the point that is being made is that being saved involves holding steadfastly to the truth revealed to us by God even when we are under pressure to abandon it, as Catholics were in the face of the Arian heresy.

The juxtaposition of this renewed warning and the preceding statement about the last judgement is not accidental. The Creed is saying that one of the key things on which will be judged at the last day is whether we have remained firm in our adherence to the Catholic faith in God the Holy Trinity and in Jesus Christ as God and Man as this has been revealed to us in Scripture and the tradition of the Church. By this it will be shown whether our heart has been right with God or not.

As Waterland says, the warnings contained in this verse, and in the Athanasian Creed as a whole, should not be understood to preclude the existence of extenuating circumstances which God will take into account at the last judgement. In his words, they are not intended:

> ... to exclude any such merciful abatement, or allowances, as shall be made: for man's particular circumstances, weaknesses, frailties, ignorance, inability, or the like; or for their sincere intentions, and honest desires of knowing, and doing the whole will of God; accompanied

---

[133] For a detailed defence of this last point see Jerry Walls, *Hell: The Logic of Eternal Damnation* (Notre Dame and London: Notre Dame Press, 1992).
[134] Kelly, *The Athanasian Creed*, 20.

with a general repentance of their sins, and a firm reliance on God's mercy, through the sole merits of Christ Jesus.[135]

However, as he goes on to say:

> There can be no doubt ... but that men are accountable for their faith, as well as for their practice: and especially if they take upon them to instruct and direct others, trusting to their own strength and parts, against the united judgement and verdict of whole churches ancient and modern.[136]

---

[135] Waterland, *A Critical History*, 150.
[136] Waterland, *A Critical History*, 150.

4. Why the Athanasian Creed Still Matters

Why It Matters to Students of History

God is eternal, but he has made human beings creatures who exist in time. Humans thus have a past, a present and a future and as individuals and communities they can only understand the present, and learn how to live well in the future, if they have a knowledge of the past.

The study of history is the way we can attain knowledge of the past beyond the scope of our own memories. Very often what people are interested in is a broad brush, or big picture, view of the past and the lessons that can be learned from this. What is often overlooked, however, is that in order to construct a reliable big picture of the past historians need first to understand accurately the smaller pieces of historical evidence on which such a big picture relies.

Knowledge of the Athanasian Creed is important for historians studying such smaller pieces of historical evidence in a variety of ways:

First, it is important for historians of Latin. As noted in chapter 1, the Athanasian Creed illustrates how the use of Latin developed in terms of vocabulary, grammar and the use of rhythm in the time between the end of the classical period and the beginning of the Middle Ages.

Secondly, it is important for historians studying the Visigothic kingdoms in Gaul and the Iberian peninsula during the fifth and sixth centuries since, as we saw in chapter 2, the Creed reveals the theological tension between the Arian Visigoths and their Catholic subjects and neighbours.

Thirdly, it is important for historians studying the development of Christian doctrine at the end of the Patristic period. It shows how the Catholic understanding of the Trinity and the Person of Christ hammered out in the theological controversies of the fourth and fifth centuries were adopted and transmitted in the life of the Church and how the teaching of Augustine was understood and employed by the theological school associated with the monastery at Lerins.

Fourthly, it is important for historians seeking to understand the roots of the continuing division between Eastern and Western Christianity. The issue of whether the Holy Spirit proceeds from the Father alone or from the Father and the Son has been one of the main theological causes for this division and verse 23 of the Athanasian Creed has been one of the key texts in the discussion of this issue.

Fifthly, it is important for historians of Christian education since it shows how the Church at the end of the Patristic period sought to help clergy and laity to understand and teach the importance and nature of Catholic orthodoxy.

Sixthly, it is important for historians of Christian liturgy since, as we saw in chapter 2, the Creed became an integral part of the Western monastic liturgical tradition and the liturgical tradition of the Church of England and Anglicanism as a whole.

Seventhly, it is important for historians seeking to understand the character of the English Reformation, since its retention by the reformed Church of England shows that the English reformers were not seeking to create a church from scratch, but to retain and make use of those aspects of the Christian tradition that were in line with the teaching of Scripture.

Finally, it is important for historians seeking to understand the development of the Church of England and the wider Anglican tradition from the seventeenth century onwards since the way that the Creed has become neglected illustrates the way in which the Anglican tradition has gradually moved away from the theology and liturgy laid down at the Reformation in response to the fact that Western culture has become more secular and averse to the ideas that theological precision matters and that God will condemn those who have turned their backs on orthodox belief.

Why It Should Matter to Those in the Church of England

The Athanasian Creed should also matter to those in the Church of England for a number of reasons.

First, as previously explained, the Creed has been an integral part of the doctrinal and liturgical history of the Church of England and of the Western Church as whole. If those in the Church of England want to understand their own history they need to understand the Creed and its place in this history.

Secondly, those clergy and laity who make the Declaration of Assent contained in Canon C.15 need to understand and be able to give their assent to the Creed because it forms part of that 'inheritance of faith' to which they affirm their loyalty as their 'inspiration and guidance under God in bringing the grace and truth of Christ to this generation and making Him known to those in you care'[137]

Thirdly, and most importantly, the Creed should matter to those in the Church of England because what it says is true.

As we saw in chapter 3, the Creed is correct when it says that adherence to the Catholic faith is vital for salvation because our belief in what God has revealed through Scripture and through the teaching of the Church faithful to Scripture (which is what the 'Catholic faith' means) is an integral part of saving faith in Christ.

Because this is the case, refusing to declare that it is so by reciting the Creed and upholding its teaching involves a failure of charity, or Christian love. As Walter Hook writes in his nineteenth-century defence of the use of the Creed against those who held that its teaching was uncharitable:

> If that be true which the Creed contains – the want of charity would be *not* in the declaration of it, but in the *refusing* to declare it. And, after all, why should men take offence at the strong expressions of the Church and the Scriptures? The assertion, or the non-assertion, does not alter the state of the case. The fact still remains as it was. If I tell a man he is dishonest, does my saying so *make* him dishonest? If he is not dishonest, he may easily convict me of slander and establish his good character. And if the Church tells a man that he is in a perilous state unless he worship one God in Trinity and Trinity in Unity, does the Church *cause* him to be in a perilous state? Instead of reviling the Church let him prove her to be in error. But if his state *be* one of peril, let him thank the Church which charitably seeks to rouse him from his security in unbelief, though she incur thereby hatred and ill-will. The charity of the Church is shown by here fearlessly maintaining the truth. By a contrary course she might become more popular; but the object of the Church

---

[137] Canon C.15, Preface at https://www.churchofengland.org/more/policy-and-thinking/canons-church- england/section-c (Accessed 8 April 2019).

is, not to please the people, but, whether they will hear or whether they will forebear, to speak God's truth.[138]

As we also saw in chapter 3, the Creed is likewise correct when it says that adherence to the Catholic faith involves believing that there is one Triune God who exists eternally as Father Son and Holy Spirit, each of whom possesses the one divine nature in all its fullness and who are distinct from each other only in their relationships to each other. It also involves believing that the Christ who was incarnate by the Holy Spirit of the Virgin Mary, who died, rose and ascended for our salvation, and who will come to be our judge, is one person who is both fully divine and fully human.

It we reject either of these beliefs what we are in fact rejecting is the very possibility of our salvation. As we have explained, it is as the one Triune God who is Father, Son and Holy Spirit, and the one Christ who is both fully human and fully divine, that God is the one who is able to save us.

As before, it is not uncharitable to declare that if someone turns away from belief in this God, then they are turning away from the only God who can save them. What would be uncharitable would be to fail to declare this.

We should recite the Creed in our liturgy and make use of it as the educational tool it was originally designed to be because when we recite the Athanasian Creed together in public worship we renew our knowledge of, and commitment to, the truths it contains and when we make it the basis for religious instruction we are taking steps to ensure that they are declared to those who do not yet know them, or who once knew them but have forgotten or rejected them.

It might be said that we do not need to make use of the Creed because we can affirm and declare the truths it contains in other ways. This is true. However, why would we not want to make use of this document which God in his providence has provided for us? Other documents set out the truths it contains, but no document does it in such a clear and concise fashion. To quote Kelly again:

---

[138] Walter Hook, *On the Use of the Athanasian Creed* (London: Forgotten books, 2018), 34. Italics original.

No other official document or creed sets forth, so incisively and with such majestic clarity, the profound theology implicit in the New Testament affirmation that 'God was in Christ reconciling the world to Himself.' And the distinctions it firmly draws are surely of lasting validity if Christianity is true at all. Notwithstanding the apparent technicality of its language, its sole concern is to assert a conception of the triune Godhead which is free from anthropomorphic polytheism, and a conception of the Incarnation which holds in tension the absolutely vital data about our Lord's divinity and humanity.[139]

In summary, the Athanasian Creed still matters today not primarily because of its historical significance, or even because of its continuing official status in the Church of England, but because of the truth of what it says. God is three in one, Christ is one person uniting two natures, who died, rose, ascended and is coming to be our judge, and we need to hold fast to these things and worship this God if we wished to be saved and to live joyfully with God for ever. Because these things are so we should understand what the Creed says, confess it ourselves and declare it to others.

In our final chapter we shall go on to look at what accepting that the Athanasian Creed matters should mean in practice.

---

[139] Kelly, *The Athanasian Creed*, 125.

5. Using the Athanasian Creed Today

Teaching the Creed in Colleges and Courses

As was noted in chapter 2, the Athanasian Creed was historically used in the training of the clergy and it should be restored to this role. If those in the Church of England are going to understand and confess the Athanasian Creed and declare it to others, then the process needs to start in the theological colleges and courses where the clergy and lay ministers are trained.

As we noted in the last chapter, the Athanasian Creed forms part of the inheritance of faith which authorised Church of England ministers promise to use as their 'inspiration and guidance' in their ministry. However, even though this is the case, clergy and lay ministers do not appear to be being trained to understand and use it.

No data appears to be available about the teaching of the Creed in theological colleges and courses, but anecdotal evidence suggests that it is almost entirely ignored, or at best referred as if it were a document of purely antiquarian interest, a statement of faith that used to be used, but is not used anymore.

What should be happening as a minimum is that all students should be introduced to what the Athanasian Creed teaches and why this teaching matters. They should also be encouraged to explore creative ways to use the Athanasian Creed in the liturgy and to think about how they themselves would teach the Creed to those in their parishes and other places of ministry.

A more radical approach would be to place the Athanasian Creed at the centre of the teaching of Christian doctrine.

It could be used to explain first of all how saving faith and Christian doctrine are related, what the 'Catholic faith' involves and why it is vital that Christians believe it and are steadfast in upholding it.

The Trinitarian section of the Creed could then be used to introduce students to the Catholic faith regarding the nature of God, with the truth about God as Trinity set forth in the Athanasian Creed being shown to be the foundation for what is said about God in the Apostles' and Nicene Creeds and in the *Thirty-Nine Articles*.

The Christological section of the Creed could further be used to introduce students to the Catholic faith regarding the person and work of Christ and eschatology. As before, what is said in the Athanasian Creed about these matters could be shown to be foundation for what is said about them in the other two Creeds and in the Articles.

One downside to such an approach to the doctrine curriculum would appear to be a lack of space for ecclesiology and sacramental theology, but these could be given their proper place in relation to discussion of the saving work of Christ and the activity of the Holy Spirit. How does the ascended Christ makes his saving work effective in the lives of men and women today? By forming a people for himself who are raised to new life by him and nourished by him through word and sacrament by the activity of the Holy Spirit.

As with the first approach, students should also be encouraged to think how they would use the Creed in the liturgy and in the instruction of those for whom they have pastoral responsibility.

In order for either of these approaches to the teaching of the Athanasian Creed to take place, those with influence over the curriculum in particular colleges or courses would need to argue for such an approach to be adopted, or action would be need to be taken at a national level to get the Ministry Division to make such an approach a required part of ministerial training. Because resources to support such a change in ministerial training do not currently exist they would need to be produced.

Using the Creed in the Parishes and Other Places of Ministry

Given the importance of the Athanasian Creed for the reasons discussed in this book, it needs to become a regular part of the life of Church of England parishes and other places where Church of England ministry takes place.

For this to happen it will first of all need to be introduced to the congregation, or congregations, involved so that people understand what the Creed is and why it matters. This could be done through a sermon series, or through a home group teaching course, or through both.

Whichever approach is adopted, those responsible for the teaching involved will themselves need to understand the Creed thoroughly and will need to be available to answer the questions which people will inevitably have, not only about the sections of the Creed linking salvation to holding firm to the Catholic faith, but about its teaching on the Trinity and the person of Christ.

At the beginning of the course, whatever form it takes, there will need to be an introduction that makes clear to people why the course is taking place, why it is important that they engage with it, and who they should go to see if they have additional questions.

It is possible to get hold of introductions and commentaries on the Creed written in the past and there are some contemporary online resources available (some of which are listed in the bibliography at the end of this study). However, unlike in the case of the Apostles', or even the Nicene Creed, the existing resources are few in number and the more detailed studies are generally dated in the issues they address. There is therefore an urgent need for more resources to be produced to support churches in teaching the Creed, but until this happens churches will need to be prepared to produce their own materials.

Because of the importance of the Athanasian Creed, requests should be made for the dioceses and the Church of England nationally to produce resources and training courses on teaching the Creed in the same way that resources and training courses are made available on other matters that are seen as important. Should the dioceses and the national Church fail to respond to such a request, approaches such be made to other organisations within the Church such as the Church Pastoral Aid Society, Forward in Faith, New Wine, or Church Society.

Once people in a church are familiar with the Creed and its importance the time would then be right to begin to recite the Creed in the liturgy. An obvious time to start doing this would be in a service at the end of the course on the Creed. The Creed could then be used on an occasional basis with a move to regular use following once congregations were familiar with using it.

For those churches who still use the *Book of Common Prayer* as their standard liturgical text the obvious thing to do in the long term would be to return to the pattern for the recitation of the Creed which the Prayer Book rubric lays down. It would also make sense to use the Prayer Book version of the Creed.

For those churches who use *Common Worship* the proper way forward would be to use the provision in *Common Worship* for the Athanasian Creed to be used in place of the Nicene Creed at Holy Communion. How often this should happen, and at which services, is an issue for local judgement, but in general the principle should be that the Athanasian Creed should be used at services where most people are likely to be familiar with it and therefore able to benefit from reciting it. Using the Creed at a service where it was alien to most people present would not be sensible.

Unfortunately there is currently no modern English translation of the Creed authorised for use by the Church of England. The Liturgical Commission should be asked to provide one, but until it does the translation in the *English Prayer Book* given in Appendix 1 would be a good one to use.[140]

Reciting all forty-two verses of the Creed together might seem a bit monotonous, so consideration should be given to saying it antiphonally. A helpful Lutheran example of how this might work is given in Appendix 2. If a church has a sufficiently strong musical tradition, singing or chanting the Creed might also be worth considering. The Royal School of Church Music[141] or the Jubilate Group[142] could be approached for help with this. For those who appreciate nineteenth century choral music there are settings of the Creed by John Stainer,[143] John Lord[144] and Edward Birch.[145]

As in the case with running teaching courses on the Creed, requests should be made to the dioceses, to the Church of England nationally, or to other bodies within the Church for resources and training on using the Athanasian Creed in worship. As it is one of the three historic Creeds

---

[140] *An English Prayer Book* is available online at the Church Society website (http://churchsociety.org/resources/page/an_english_prayer_book) and its text can be freely reproduced providing where it came from is properly noted.
[141] Royal School of Church Music, www.rscm.org.uk.
[142] Jubilate Group, https://jubilatemusic.com.
[143] John Stainer, *The Ancient Plain Song of the Athanasian Creed arranged for voices in unison* (London: Novello, Ewer & Co., 1886).
[144] John Lord, *The Athanasian Creed Pointed to the Seventh Tone* (London: Novello, Ewer & Co., 1894).
[145] Edward Birch, *Athanasian Creed in G* (London: Novello, 1894).

authorised for use in Church of England worship, resources and training should be made available.

It is also important that teaching courses on what the Creed is and why it matters should be held on a regular basis for the sake of people joining the church and that appropriate forms of teaching about the Creed should be provided for young people as part of their catechesis. There is no reason why teenagers should not be able to comprehend what the Creed teaches and why it matters, but the instruction given to them about this will need to fit into the overall pattern of teaching provided for them and those responsible for this teaching should be given help and resources on how to teach them about the Creed.

The final point to note is that none of the above will happen unless people take action to make them happen. Therefore it is not enough for us to believe that the Athanasian Creed should be used more in the Church of England and to wish that it were so. We need to take steps to bring this about. It follows that if you have read this book and agree with what it says, you need to spend time with God prayerfully considering what action he wants you to take and then take it.

Over to you ...

Appendix 1: The Athanasian Creed from the *English Prayer Book*

Whosoever wishes to be saved

before all things it is necessary that he hold the catholic faith,
which faith, if anyone does not keep it whole and unharmed,
without doubt he will perish everlastingly.

Now, the catholic faith is this,
that we worship one God in Trinity, and Trinity in Unity,
neither confusing the Persons
nor dividing the divine Being.

For there is one Person of the Father, another of the Son,
and another of the Holy Spirit,
but the Godhead of the Father, the Son and the Holy Spirit is all one,
their glory equal, their majesty co-eternal.
Such as the Father is, such is the Son
and such is the Holy Spirit:
the Father uncreated, the Son uncreated
and the Holy Spirit uncreated;
the Father infinite, the Son infinite
and the Holy Spirit infinite;
the Father eternal, the Son eternal
and the Holy Spirit eternal;
and yet they are not three Eternals
but one Eternal,
just as they are not three Uncreateds, nor three Infinites,
but one Uncreated and one Infinite.

In the same way, the Father is almighty, the Son almighty
and the Holy Spirit almighty;
and yet they are not three Almighties
but one Almighty.
Thus the Father is God, the Son is God
and the Holy Spirit is God;
and yet there are not three Gods
but one God.
Thus the Father is the Lord, the Son is the Lord,

and the Holy Spirit is the Lord;
and yet not three Lords
but one Lord.

Because, just as we are compelled by Christian truth
to confess each Person singly to be both God and Lord,
so are we forbidden by the catholic religion
to say, There are three Gods, or three Lords.
The Father is from none,
not made nor created nor begotten;
the Son is from the Father alone,
not made nor created, but begotten:
the Holy Spirit is from the Father and the Son,
not made nor created nor begotten, but proceeding.
So there is one Father, not three Fathers; one Son, not three Sons;
one Holy Spirit, not three Holy Spirits.
And in this Trinity there is no before or after,
no greater or less,
but all three Persons are co-eternal with each other
and co-equal.

So that in all things, as has already been said,
the Trinity in Unity, and Unity in Trinity, is to be worshipped.
He therefore who wishes to be saved
let him think thus of the Trinity.

Furthermore, it is necessary to everlasting salvation
that he should faithfully believe the incarnation of
our Lord Jesus Christ.
Now, the right faith is that we should believe and confess
that our Lord Jesus Christ, the Son of God,
is both God and man equally.

He is God from the Being of the Father, begotten before the worlds,
and he is man from the being of his mother, born in the world;
perfect God and perfect man,
having both man's rational soul and human flesh;
equal to the Father as regards his divinity
and inferior to the Father as regards his humanity;

who, although he is God and man,
yet he is not two, but one Christ;
one, however, not by conversion of the Godhead into flesh
but by the taking up of humanity into God;
utterly one, not by confusion of human and divine being
but by unity of Christ's one Person.

For just as the rational soul and flesh are one man,
so God and man are one Christ;
who suffered for our salvation,
descended to the realm of the dead,
rose again the third day from the dead,
ascended to heaven, sat down at the right hand of the Father,
from where he will come to judge the living and the dead;
at whose coming all men will rise again with their bodies
and will give an account for their own actions,
and those who have done good will go into life everlasting
and those who have done evil into everlasting fire.

This is the catholic faith
which, if anyone does not believe it faithfully and firmly,
he cannot be saved.[146]

---

[146] Text from *An English Prayer Book*, 'Athanasian Creed,' at http://archive.churchsociety.org/publications/EnglishPrayerBook/EPB_AthanasianCreed.asp (Accessed 8 April 2019).

Appendix 2: A Lutheran Antiphonal version of the Athanasian Creed

The Athanasian Creed

Whoever will be saved shall, above all else, hold the catholic faith. **Which faith, except everyone keeps whole and undefiled, without doubt he will perish eternally.**

And the catholic faith is this, that we worship one God in Three Persons and Three Persons in one God, **neither confusing the Persons nor dividing the substance.**

For there is One Person of the Father, another of the Son, and another of the Holy Spirit. **But the Godhead of the Father, of the Son, and of the Holy Spirit is all one: the glory equal, the majesty coeternal.**

Such as the Father is, such is the Son, and such is the Holy Spirit. **The Father uncreated, the Son uncreated, the Holy Spirit uncreated.**

The Father incomprehensible, the Son incomprehensible, the Holy Spirit incomprehensible. **The Father eternal, the Son eternal, the Holy Spirit eternal.** And yet They are not three eternals **but One Eternal.**

As there are not three uncreated nor three incomprehensibles
but One Uncreated and One Incomprehensible.

So likewise the Father is almighty, the Son almighty, and the Holy Spirit almighty.

And yet They are not three almighties but One Almighty.
So the Father is God, the Son is God, and the Holy Spirit is God.
And yet They are not three Gods but one God.
So likewise the Father is Lord, the Son Lord, and the Holy Spirit Lord.
And yet They are not three Lords but One Lord.

For as we are compelled by the Christian truth to acknowledge every Person by Himself to be both God and Lord,
So we cannot by the catholic faith say that there are three Gods or three Lords.

The Father is made of none,
neither created nor begotten.
The Son is of the Father alone,
not made nor created but begotten.
The Holy Spirit is of the Father and of the Son,
neither made nor created nor begotten but proceeding.
So there is One Father, not three Fathers; One Son, not three Sons;

One Holy Spirit, not three Holy
Spirits.

**And in this Trinity none is
before or after another; none
is greater or less than another;**
but the whole three Persons are
coeternal together and coequal, so
that in all things, as is aforesaid,
**the Unity in Trinity and the
Trinity in Unity is to be
worshiped.**

He, therefore, that will be saved is
compelled thus to think of the Trinity.
**Furthermore, it is necessary to
everlasting salvation that he also
believe faithfully the incarnation
of our Lord Jesus Christ.**

For the right faith is that we believe
and confess that our Lord Jesus
Christ, the Son of God,
is God and man;
God of the substance of the Father,
begotten before the worlds;
**and man of the substance of His
mother, born in the world.**

Perfect God and perfect man, of a reasonable
soul and human flesh subsisting.
**Equal to the Father as touching
His Godhead and inferior to the
Father as touching His
manhood;**
Who, although He is God and man,
**yet He is not two but One
Christ:**
One, not by conversion of the

Godhead into flesh but by taking the manhood into God;
One altogether, not by confusion of substance but by unity of Person.

For as the reasonable soul and flesh is one man,
so God and man is One Christ;
Who suffered for our salvation, descended into hell, rose again the third day from the dead.
He ascended into heaven, He sits at the right hand of the Father, God Almighty, from whence He will come to judge the living and the dead—
At whose coming all men will rise again with their bodies and will give an account of their own works.
And they that have done good will go into life everlasting; and they that have done evil, into everlasting fire.

This is the catholic faith which, except a man believe faithfully and firmly,
he cannot be saved.[147]

---

[147] 'The Athanasian Creed' at http://www.xrysostom.com/theology/athcreed.pdf (Accessed 8 April 2019).

Bibliography

Books and articles on the Athanasian Creed

Joshua Bennett, 'The Age of Athanasius, The Church of England and the Athanasian Creed 1870–1873,' *Church History and Religious Culture*, 97, 2017.

Walter Hook, *On the use of the Athanasian Creed* (London: Forgotten books, 2018).

J N D Kelly, *The Athanasian Creed* (London: A&C Black, 1964).

Malcom Maccoll, *The Damnatory Clauses of the Athanasian Creed* (Collingwood: Trieste Publishing, 2017).

G Morin, 'L'Origine du symbole d'Athanase: temoignage inedit de s. Cesaire d'Arles,' (*Revue Benedictine*, XLIV, 1932), 207–219.

G W D Ommanney, *A Critical Dissertation on the Athanasian Creed* (Oxford: OUP, 1897).

J Hamer Rawdon, *The Athanasian Creed, Six Expository Addresses* (Collingwood: Trieste Publishing, 2017.)

A P Stanley, 'The Athanasian Creed,' *Contemporary Review*, 15, 1870.

Daniel Waterland, *A critical history of the Athanasian Creed*, (London: Forgotten Books, 2015).

Web resources

The Athanasian Creed at
http://www.xrysostom.com/theology/athcreed.pdf

An English Prayer Book, 'Athanasian Creed,' at http://archive.churchsociety.org/publications/EnglishPrayerBook/EPB_AthanasianCreed.asp.

ATP Good works in the Athanasian Creed? at
https://www.youtube.com/watch?v=QVqSnQ9-PGw

Church Society – The Athanasian Creed at http://www.churchsociety.org/issues_new/doctrine/creeds/iss_doctrine_creeds_athanasianabout.asp.

Book of Concord at http://bookofconcord.org/creeds.php

Gallican Confession at https://cfcreforme.blogspot.com/2007/11/gallican-confession-of-faith-1559.html

The Jerusalem Statement at https://www.gafcon.org/resources/the-complete-jerusalem-statement

The Athanasian Creed – Doctrine of the Trinity at https://www.youtube.com/watch?v=4lQFYyvxTwE

Theological Statement of the Anglican Church of North America at http://www.anglicanchurch.net/index.php/main/Theology/

To be a Christian at http://anglicanchurch.net/?/main/catechism

Trinities 002 – The Athanasian Creed at https://www.youtube.com/watch?v=rQYHPXF9EOU

Other Studies

Karl Barth, *Church Dogmatics* I/1 (London and New York: T&T Clark, 2004).

Karl Barth, Church Dogmatics, IV/1 (London and New York: T&T Clark, 2004).

Karl Barth *Dogmatics in Outline* (London: SCM, 1985).

Gerald Bray, *The Faith We Confess* (London: Latimer Trust, 2009).

W Beveridge, *Ecclesia Anglicana, Ecclesia Catholica* (Oxford: OUP, 1846).

Bibliography

Harold Browne, *An Exposition of the Thirty Nine Articles* (London: John Parker, 1860).

A E Burn, *An Introduction to the Creeds and to the Te Deum* (London: Methuen, 1899).

The Church of England Doctrine Commission, *The Doctrine of Salvation* (London: CHP, 1995),

Norman Davies, *Forgotten Kingdoms* (London: Penguin, 2012).

James, DolezaL, *God without Parts* (Eugene: Pickwick, 2011).

Steven Duby, *Divine Simplicity* (London and New York, T&T Clark, 2016).

John M Frame, *Apologetics: A Justification of Christian Belief* (Phillipsburg: Presbyterian and Reformed Publishing, 2015).

E C S Gibson, *The Thirty Nine Articles of the Church of England* (London: Methuen, 3ed, 1902).

W H Griffith Thomas, *The Principles of Theology* (London: Church Book Room Press, 1951).

Anthony Hanson and Richard Hanson, *Reasonable Faith* (Oxford: OUP, 1981).

Richard Hooker, *The Laws of Ecclesiastical Polity* (Oxford: OUP, 1849).

Philip Hughes, *The Second Epistle to the Corinthians* (Grand Rapids: Eerdmans, 1962).

J N D Kelly, *Early Christian Doctrines,* 5ed (London: A&C Black, 1980).

C S Lewis, *The Four Loves* (Glasgow: Fontana, 1965).

J R Lumby, *The History of the Creeds* (Cambridge: Deighton Bell, 1873).

Martin Luther, *A Commentary on St. Paul's Epistle to the* Galatians (Cambridge: James Clarke, 1978).

George Miller, *Observations on the Doctrines of Christianity, in Reference to Arianism, Illustrating the Moderation of the Established Church* (London: Rivington, 1825).

Michael Ovey, *Your Will Be Done* (London: Latimer Trust, 2016).

J I Packer, *Knowing God* (London: Hodder and Stoughton, 1973).

John Pearson, *An Exposition of the Creed*, Art XVIII (London: George Bell, 1902).

H M Relton, *A Study in Christology* (London: SPCK, 1934).

Peter Sanlon, *Simply God* (Nottingham: IVP, 2014).

Tom Smail, *The Giving Gift* (London: Hodder and Stoughton, 1988).

C A Swainson, The Nicene and Apostles' Creeds (London: John Murray, 1875).

John V Taylor, *The Go-Between God* (London: SCM, 1975).

C H Turner, *The History of Creeds and Anathemas in the Early Church* (London: SPCK, 1906).

Jerry L Walls, *Hell: the Logic of Eternal Damnation* (Notre Dame and London: Notre Dame Press, 1992).

Christopher Watkin, *Thinking Through Creation* (Phillipsburg: Presbyterian and Reformed Publishing, 2017).

Patristic Texts

Athanasius, *On the Incarnation of the Word*, In the *Nicene and Post-Nicene Fathers* (Edinburgh and Grand Rapids: T&T Clark/Eerdmans, 1998).

BIBLIOGRAPHY

Athanasius, *The Orations of St Athanasius against the Arians* (London: Macmillan, 1873).

Athenagoras, *A plea for the Christians* in *The Ante-Nicene Fathers* (Edinburgh and Grand Rapids: T&T Clark/Eerdmans, 2001).

Augustine: *Anti-Pelagian Writings*, in the *Nicene and Post-Nicene Fathers* (Edinburgh and Grand Rapids: T&T Clark/Eerdmans, 1997.).

Augustine, *Enchiridion on Faith, Hope and Love* in *The Nicene and Post Nicene Fathers*, First Series, Vol. III (Edinburgh and Grand Rapids: T&T Clark/Eerdmans).

Augustine, *On the Trinity* in *The Nicene & Post Nicene Fathers* Vol III (Edinburgh and Grand Rapids: T&T Clark/Eerdmans, 1998).

Augustine, *The City of God* (Harmondsworth: Penguin, 1981).

Gregory of Tours, *The History of the Franks* (London: Penguin Books, 1974).

Irenaeus, *Against Heresies*, The Ante-Nicene Fathers, Vol.1, (Edinburgh and Grand Rapids, T&T Clark/Eerdmans, 1996).

John of Damascus, *Exposition of the Orthodox Faith* in *The Nicene and Post Nicene Fathers* 2nd series, vol. IX (Grand Rapids: Eerdmans, 1997).

Anglican Foundations Series

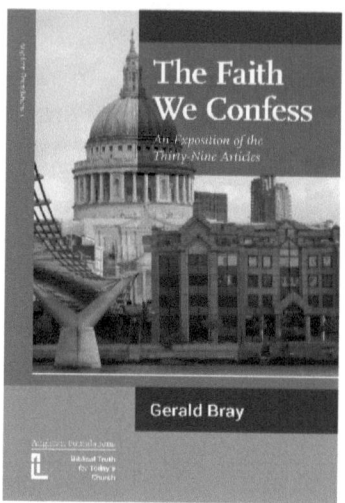

The Anglican Foundations series are a collection of books which offer practical guidance on Church of England services.

These include:
- The Faith We Confess – An exposition of the Thirty-Nine Articles
- The 'Very Pure Word of God – The Book of Common Prayer as a model of biblical liturgy
- Dearly Beloved – Building God's people through morning and evening prayer
- Day by Day – The rhythm of the Bible in the Book of Common Prayer
- The Supper – Cranmer and Communion
- A Fruitful Exhortation – A guide to the Homilies
- Instruction in the Way of the Lord – A guide to the catechism
- Till Death Do Us Part – "The solemnization of Matrimony" in the Book of Common Prayer
- Sure and Certain Hope – Death and burial
- The Athanasian Creed

Recently Released by the Latimer Trust

Synods by *Gerald Bray*

Synods are gatherings of church officers that convene for the purpose of deliberating what church policy should be. Their agenda may include resolving disputes that have arisen as well, as making plans for the future development of the life of the church.

They are typically representative bodies, though who they represent varies from time to time and from church to church. They have been held from the very earliest days of Christianity, and for many centuries they were understood to be assemblies of bishops. That is still the case in the Roman Catholic and Eastern Orthodox churches, but Anglican practice is much broader in scope, including clergy and laity as well. Modern synods also meet on a regular basis and operate according to a fixed constitution. They share some features in common with those of other times and places, but they are not direct descendants of any particular ancient tradition. There is no form of Anglican synodical government beyond the level of the national church, a fact that has become increasingly problematic in the worldwide Anglican Communion. Reform of the national synodical structure and the development of an effective form of synodical government that will be regarded as authoritative by the entire Communion are the greatest challenges we face today and it is these that this essay seeks to address.

Lex Orandi, Lex Credendi by *Martin Davie*

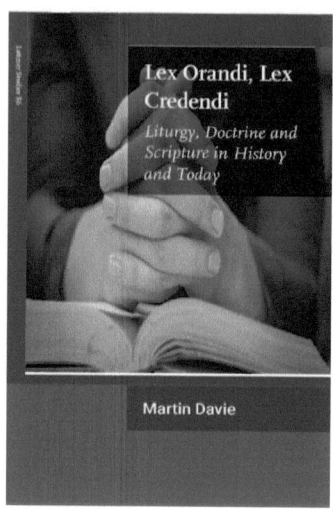

The Latin phrase lex orandi, lex credendi ('the law of praying is the law of believing') is a phrase which is often used in Anglican theological discussion, but which needs careful unpacking if its meaning is to be properly understood.

In this study Martin Davie provides such unpacking. He traces the history of the phrase back to its origins in the work of St. Prosper of Aquitaine in the fifth century, explains what it means and gives examples of how it has been both used and misused in the Roman Catholic, Orthodox and Anglican traditions.

His conclusion is that when it is rightly understood the principle lex orandi, lex credendi provides a useful tool for assessing both a church's liturgy and its doctrine. It reminds us that a church's liturgical practice needs to cohere with its doctrine and both need to be in line with Scripture.

He also argues that the use of this tool shows us that not only are proposals for marking same-sex relationships unacceptable, but so also is the new proposal to use liturgy to mark gender transition.

www.ingramcontent.com/pod-product-compliance
Ingram Content Group UK Ltd.
Pitfield, Milton Keynes, MK11 3LW, UK
UKHW041305180426
11947UKWH00009B/706